THE WORLD'S MOST
CHILLING TALES
FROM BEYOND
THE GRAVE

THE WORLD'S MOST
CHILLING TALES
FROM BEYOND
THE GRAVE

BY
NIGEL BLUNDELL

SUNBURST BOOKS

PHOTOGRAPHY

Every effort has been made to trace the ownership of
all copyright material and to secure permission from copyright
holders. In the event of any question arising as to the use of
any material we will be pleased to make the necessary
corrections in future printings.

Text © Nigel Blundell 1996
Design © Sunburst Books 1996

This edition published 1996 by
Sunburst Books
Kiln House,
210 New Kings Road,
London
SW6 4NZ

ISBN 1 85778 156 2

Printed and bound in Great Britain

Contents

INTRODUCTION

Nothing is more intriguing than a good mystery story. Within these pages we present the ultimate in mysteries – stories that have no ending, no neat and final solution. We tell tales of extraordinary phenomena, of marvel and enigma. Accounts of events and experiences that are truly outside our understanding.

We enter the realms of the paranormal, where voices from other worlds guide or haunt us here in the present.

From vampires to werewolves to spirits and angels, from jinxes and curses to premonitions to prophecy – this book examines the most impenetrable, timeless, enigmatic mysteries.

How, for instance, can a king's curse reach from beyond the grave? What makes a statue weep blood? How can voodoo bring a zombie back from the dead? Can we receive messages from Heaven?

As Stephen King and Stephen Spielberg have discovered, an eerie mystery yarn cannot fail to enthral. The stories in this book, however, beat the plots of any mere thriller.

For these are mysteries no fiction writer could make up; and which no reader has ever solved!

VAMPIRES

They call them the living dead – the black cloaked shadows that swoop on sleeping humans. They are the personification of evil, the very essence of our worst nightmares. They strike in the deepest hours of darkness. They have no pity, no souls, no morals, no mercy. They are... VAMPIRES!

What sets the vampire apart from every other supernatural creature of the night is that it drinks the blood of living beings. Sceptics may blame Hollywood for the creation of such demons, but the truth is that the fear of blood-sucking monsters has been around since the earliest recorded history.

Some academics have dated the start of legends about the living dead who feed upon human blood at around 500 to 600 BC in ancient China. But the early Babylonians and Persians, the ancient peoples of India, the Malaysians and the Polynesians, the Aztecs and even the Eskimos have all built this strange phobia into their cultures.

It was not until the birth of Christianity, however, that the spirit of vampirism seems to have crept across Europe and created in the psyche of its simple people the sort of feared figure we now understand.

When the early Christians taught how Christ's

Castle Brau in Romania, the home of Dracula.

blood had saved humanity, it was difficult to prevent pagans taking the recuperative powers of blood literally and returning to human sacrifice as a means of rejuvenation. In 11th century Europe, the blood of virgins was still being prescribed by alchemists for its healing and rejuvenating effects.

The other Christian belief that encouraged superstition was that sinners' souls can be saved by being given the last rites. This meant that those who had been excommunicated or had committed suicide were unable to reach Heaven. These lost souls – revenants, as they are known – could return to haunt the living.

They normally return in a harmless form, unseen and untouchable. Early Christians, however, believed that a certain species could 'return in body'. These were the truly damned, who had managed to escape the afterlife and become parasites on the living.

Two early English works of literature reveal the general acceptance of the existence of the 'undead'. *Historia Rerum Anglicarum* (On England) by William of Newburgh and *De Nugis Curialium* (Courtiers' Triflings) by Walter Map, both written in the late 12th century, tell how the excommunicated dead leave their coffins to torment and murder those who were once close to them. William of Newburgh, who was an Augustinian monk, advocated the reopening of tombs in day-

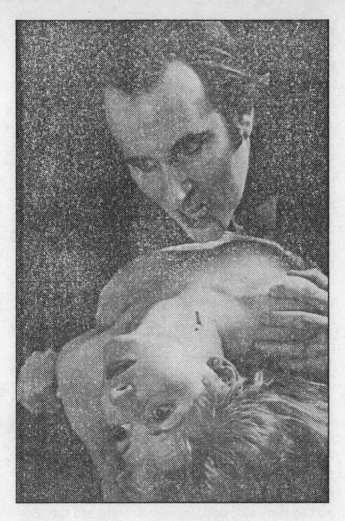

Titillation and terror - the vampire's kiss.

light to trap these monsters. A sign of guilt was that the corpse was still intact but spattered with blood. Such a body should be pierced with a sword and burned.

A name was coined at this time for these dead-and-alive creatures: *cadaver sanguisugus* (blood-sucking corpse). The legend of the vampire had been born.

In the 14th century, bubonic plague caused hasty burials throughout Europe, often in hurried, mass graves and sometimes at the nearest roadside spot outside town. Some of the victims were still alive when nailed into their coffins. Suddenly there were cases galore of vampires who had awoken from the grave – and so the vampire legend was spread by a frightened, superstitious people.

Vampires supposedly spread their evil by biting mortals in their sleep and, once bitten, the transformation from man to fiend would begin immediately. The bite of a vampire is fatal – although after assignment to a coffin, the victim soon takes on the powers of vampirism and starts clawing his or her way out at night. After partaking of a little blood-gorging themselves, the new vampire's face turns from ghostly white to healthy pink, the lips as crimson as their last meal.

Prime candidates for this ghoulish life are said to be suicides and excommunicants. For years it was the custom in England to bury them at crossroads to save them from becoming vampires. Such makeshift burials became so common, and were so fraught with health hazards, that parliament banned the practice in 1824.

Astral projection – the phenomenon by which the soul is said to rise from the body and float freely across the earth at fantastic speed – was also said to put the shell left behind in great danger of being taken over by a vampire. This belief reinforced the old European custom of guarding a body from occupation by spirits if death occurred between Christmas and Epiphany, a time when the forces of evil have much greater power on Earth.

Other folklore paths to possession included sleeping outdoors with the full moon shining straight on your face, or conceiving a child on the night of the full moon.

Over the centuries, legends such as these spread from central European regions such as Prussia, Silesia and Bohemia, to France, England, Italy, Spain and Portugal. In the early 1500s Protestant teachers like Martin Luther and John Calvin well knew the curse of these evil spirits. Ironically, both Catholic and Protestant leaders vied in their efforts to stamp out heresy in all its forms by the cruellest means imaginable.

In the 17th century, vampire fever reached Greece, Bulgaria, Albania and Russia. But it was the following century that saw an epidemic of vampire-hunting, which coincided with further outbreaks of bubonic plague.

The classic description of these creatures was given by a German theologian, Johann Heinrich Zopf, in 1733. He wrote:

'Vampires issue forth from their graves in the night, attack people sleeping quietly in their beds, suck out all the blood from their bodies and destroy them. They beset men, women and children alike, sparing neither age nor sex. Those who are under the fatal malignity of their influence complain of suffocation and a total deficiency of spirits, after which they soon expire.'

One single case spread vampire fever across all of 18th century Europe. It followed the death in 1726 of a Serbian peasant named Arnold Paole, who had fallen from a hay wagon. Ever after, the villagers of Medvegia were terrorised by a blood-sucking beast who killed or maimed humans and animals alike. Paole was the main suspect and the villagers decided to dig up his coffin. An Austrian military doctor, Johann Fluckinger, who had been sent to investigate, wrote this report:

'The man had during his lifetime often revealed that he had been troubled by a vampire, wherefore he had eaten from the earth of the vampire's grave and had smeared himself with the vampire's blood, in order to be free of the vexation he had suffered. After his death some people complained that they were being bothered by this same Arnold Paole, and four people were killed by him. In order to end this evil, they dug up Paole 40 days after his death.

'They found that he was quite complete and undecayed, and that fresh blood had flowed from his eyes, nose, mouth and ears; that the old nails on his hands and feet, along with the skin, had fallen off, and that new ones had grown; and since they saw from this that he was a true vampire, they drove a stake through his heart, according to their custom, whereby he gave an audible groan and bled copiously. Thereupon they burned the body to ashes.

'These same people say further that all those who were tortured and killed by the vampires must themselves become vampires. Therefore they disinterred the above mentioned four people in the same way.'

Ennemoser's *History of Magic* in 1854 elaborated upon the story:

'It was seen that the corpse had moved to one side, the jaws gaped wide open and the blue lips were moist with new blood which had trickled in a thin stream from a corner of the mouth. All unafraid, the old sexton caught the body and twisted it straight. "So you have not wiped your mouth since last night's work," he cried.

'The vampire looked indeed as though he had

not been dead a day. On handling the corpse, the scarfskin came off and below that were new skin and new nails.'

According to the mid-European rule books, the correct method employed to identify a buried vampire was rather elaborate. A young virgin had to be mounted on a virgin horse (only pure black or white would suffice) and ride through the graveyard. The horse would rear up at the tainted tomb!

Having once uncovered the vampire, he must be disposed of by sharpening a stake of aspen (the wood used for Jesus's cross) or hawthorn (his crown of thorns) and plunging it into the fiend's heart as he lies in his coffin. Garlic may also be spread about as an added defence.

That much is probably now known even by most children. For which we owe much to the author Bram Stoker who, in 1897, published his startling novel *Dracula*, which renewed the morbid fascination for vampires in the western world. Stoker's inspiration for his thriller was Vlad Tepes – 'Vlad the Impaler' – who inflicted bloody tortures on both his enemies and his own countrymen in Walachia (now part of Romania) in the 15th century. From the moment *Dracula* hit the bookshelves there was no looking back for this most feared of all supernatural night stalkers.

It took only the invention of cinematography and the vivid imagination of the 20th century movie

A woodcut of the real life Dracula - Count Vlad the Impaler.

makers to enshrine Dracula and his vampire fiends in a horror hall of fame. Sceptics may blame Hollywood for creating a modern myth but, as we have seen, vampires have been around for a lot longer than most people think – and show no signs of dying just yet!

VOODOO

The summer of 1918 showed every sign of being a record-breaker for Haiti's sugar cane plantations. There was a shortage of labour and growers were ready to hire almost anybody to ensure that the bumper crop was brought in on time. So when a group of scruffy labourers presented themselves at the Haitian-American Sugar Corporation (HASCO), the manager overcame his reservations and put them to work. He didn't believe they would be very productive but they were better than nothing. Besides he knew their head man, Ti Joseph. Joseph would be anxious to get every penny of the bonus on offer.

Joseph said his men were from an isolated village near the Dominican Republic border. They were nervous because they had never travelled so far from their homes. But they would work well, provided they did not mix with other labourers. By the end of the first day, the HASCO boss was delighted. Ti Joseph's gang had brought in the day's biggest quantity of cane, yet seemed far from exhausted.

And so the pattern was set for the week ahead. Each day the strong, silent human workhorses would out-harvest every other team in the plantation, and each night they would retire to their own rough quarters to eat and sleep. It was not until Sunday – a rest day – that their secret was laid bare. That day Ti Joseph pocketed his bonus and headed for the bars and clubs of Port-au-Prince.

His wife, Constance, felt it was wrong to leave the men lolling aimlessly about and so she invited them to attend a church festival nearby. As a special treat, she issued each of them with a packet of biscuits and some nuts. Cautiously they started to eat. Within minutes there was an extraordinary transformation. The workers burst into tears and started screaming. Then in a confused, panicky state they began heading back to their home village.

Days later they found their families in what must go down as one of history's most bizarre reunions. Incredibly, each member of the plantation team had died and been buried within the previous few months. It seemed they had been targeted by a voodoo witch doctor who had raised them from the dead and turned them into zombies. Somehow, the abrupt change in their diet had broken the spell.

This account, researched and published by the US explorer and writer William Seabrook, was backed by a number of witnesses. But it is by no means an isolated incident. Haiti is full of stories about the mysterious power of voodoo and the curse of the zombies, many of which date from the recent past.

One of the most inhuman voodoo practitioners of all time was Adolfo de Jesus Constanzo. Born in Miami of Cuban extraction, he studied the black magic arts of Palo Mayombe, a vicious and violent sect imported from the Congo. The cult believes the spirits of the dead exist in limbo and can be harnessed if the gods are regularly appeased with the fresh blood of human sacrifices. Constanzo would keep a cauldron constantly filled with blood and, most importantly, the skull of a human who had died a violent death. The more painful and horrific the death, the more potent the spell that the high priest can cast.

At the age of 21, Constanzo moved to Mexico City where in 1983 he began to pursue a vocation as a Palo Mayombe priest. Superstitious drugs barons turned to him for magical protection at $50,000 a spell. As a consequence, his cauldron needed constant replenishment with fresh blood and skulls, and decapitated corpses were regularly fished out of rivers and lakes.

In 1987 Constanzo fell out with a gang led by Guillermo Calzada. Shortly afterwards Calzada, his wife, his mother, his partner, his secretary, his maid and his bodyguard were all dragged from a river. All seven had been dreadfully mutilated before being killed. Their fingers and toes and, in the case of the men, their genitals, had been sliced off. Their heads were also missing – gone to feed the cauldron.

Constanzo moved his voodoo circle to Matamoros, near the Texan border, where in 1988 he tortured and ritually sacrificed at least 13 people. His method was to beat his victim severely before cutting off the nose, ears, fingers, toes and genitals. The poor wretch would then be partially flayed. Finally, still alive, his skull would be split open over the bubbling cauldron.

It was essential to the success of the ceremony that there should be as much pain as possible and the victim should die screaming. The spirit had to be confused and terrified as it left the body, making it easier to subjugate.

In March 1989 a group of American students crossed the border from Texas for a night of cheap booze. Mark Kilroy, a 21-year-old medical student, was kidnapped, driven to Constanzo's hideout and hideously butchered. The ensuing manhunt eventually tracked Constanzo back to Mexico City, where he died in a police shootout.

In 1936, a woman called Felicia Felix-Mentor turned up lost and confused in the Artibonite Valley area of Haiti. She seemed uncomprehending of those around her and bore strange scars on her eyelids which looked like burns. But although she was not sure of her identity, plenty of the locals were. They remembered her well – because they had attended her funeral two years earlier.

The Felix-Mentor case attracted world media

Adolfo de Jesus Constanzo.

coverage because it offered the first hard evidence that zombies were not merely the product of a simple, superstitious society.

Felix-Mentor was interviewed by one of the most respected academics of her time, the ethnographer Zora Hurston, who spent days with her patient trying to unlock the secrets buried deep in her psyche.

Hurston remained puzzled by what had happened, though she didn't doubt the truth of the tale. She concluded that zombiefication was a method of administering fast-acting poisons on a victim, and that those deemed to have betrayed the teachings of the voodoo religion became targets for revenge.

For hundreds of years, Haiti has been held in the grip of voodoo, and even today many still run their lives by it. The religion has increased the power of a few witch doctors while preventing the peasantry as a whole from educating itself.

No one knows exactly when or how it all started. Certainly, voodoo flourished under the atrocities perpetrated by first the Spanish and later the French colonial authorities, with warrior-priests such as the mysterious Boukman marshalling a feared resistance movement. He administered potions to his fighters which were said to turn them into fearless zombies. Another rebel, Macandel, taught his followers the art of poisoning. He was later captured and burnt at the stake.

It was not until the 20th century that Haiti's most famous leaders – Dr Francois 'Papa Doc' Duvalier and his son Jean-Claude 'Baby Doc' – turned voodoo into their personal instrument of oppression. Papa Doc assumed the countenance of a high priest and established a band of thuggish enforcers called the Tontons Macoutes to ensure his word was law. Word was put about that any who challenged the Duvaliers would be transformed into zombies.

Haitians responded by adopting bizarre practices to save themselves from the black magic. Heavy boulders would be lugged onto new graves to deter witch doctors from raising the corpse into the ranks of the living dead. Families would take turns to watch a grave until they were certain the body had decomposed. Some staunch believers even machine-gunned their dead loved ones, believing that this put them beyond the reach of voodoo magic.

It was not until the 1980s that science came to the rescue of the Haitians. The celebrated anthropologist Dr E Wade Davis published a paper which laid bare the secrets of the witch doctor. One of Davis's most extraordinary conclusions was that 'zombieism actually exists – there are Haitians who have been raised from their graves and returned to life'.

Dr Davis's research, commissioned by the

principal of the Port-au-Prince Psychiatric Centre, Dr Lamarque Douyon, concentrated on a zombie called Clairvius Narcisse. Narcisse had died in the island's Albert Schweitzer Hospital of a fever in 1962, aged 40. Records showed he had been buried the next day. However, 18 years later, Narcisse approached his sister Angeline and recounted his amazing experience.

He claimed he had been turned into a zombie by a witch doctor acting on the instructions of his brothers. They were furious because he would not agree to auction off some of the family's land. Narcisse had no recollection of his time in the coffin. But he remembered being 'restored' to life by a witch doctor and told how he had been put to work on farms with other zombie slaves. The effects of the witch doctor's potion gradually wore off, allowing him to make his escape, and he wandered the country as a beggar for 16 years.

Everything about his story turned out to be true. Hospital records confirmed his claims and when his coffin was disinterred it was found to be empty. Even the zombie workforce he spoke of was tracked down and several men recalled how he had escaped.

Dr Davis suspected that witch doctors used exotic poisons to turn their subjects into a state akin to suspended animation. With no sign of breathing or a pulse, the prospective zombie would be duly certified dead and despatched for burial. A few days later the voodoo priest would exhume him, inject an antidote, and sell his victim as a slave. The longer the period between initial poisoning and exhumation, the greater the danger of brain damage. This however could be a positive advantage for the witch doctors, who wanted easily-controllable zombies.

Among the natural toxins studied by Dr Davis were those found in the plant *Datura stramonium* (also known as 'zombie's cucumber') and in species of toad and puffer fish. When he analysed 'zombie powder' used by the black magic practitioners, he identified traces of human corpse, nettle, toad and puffer fish. Davis did not claim he had all the answers. He pointed out that the art of raising a zombie from the grave involved some greater skill than simply administering an antidote. Witch doctors were also adept at dosing their victims up with further potions that kept them in their zombiefied state. This explained why a few people – perhaps with some natural resistance to the potions – managed to escape the clutches of the voodoo men.

This was Dr Davis's conclusion on the powers of voodoo witch doctors who turn their victims into zombies:

'Zombies are a Haitian phenomenon which can be explained logically. The active ingredients in the poison are extracts from the skin of the toad *bufo marinus* and one or more species of puffer fish. The skin of the toad is a natural chemical factory which produces hallucinogens, powerful anaesthetics and chemicals which affect the heart and nervous system. The puffer fish contains a deadly nerve poison called tetrodotoxin.

'A witch-doctor in Haiti is very skilled in administering just the right dose of poison. Too much poison will kill the victim completely and resuscitation will not be possible. Too little and the victim will not be a convincing corpse.'

Voodoo practices are still rife in Mexico and among the immigrant populations of Florida. The Miami River is known as the River of Chickens by the sanitation crews who, in one three-day period alone, dredged up the headless bodies of 200 chickens – all the remains of sacrifices to the spirits of the voodoo.

ANGELS

The weary British soldiers appeared to be staring defeat – and probably death – in the face. It was among the most bloody campaigns of the First World War and the courageous members of the British Expeditionary Force had not willingly given up an inch of territory to the German army. But now, they were beaten back to the Belgian border with the Kaiser's cavalry hard on their heels. The German forces were fresh, superior in number and fired up with fervour. No one and nothing seemed able to stop them.

In the eyes of the hard-pressed Tommys, the scene at the muddy field in Mons had all the hallmarks of a last stand. Some of the infantrymen were preparing to meet their maker. Many prayed. Perhaps one made a plea from the heart for the intervention of St George, the patron saint of England. What happened next on that bleak afternoon at the end of August 1914 left all of them in awe.

A heavenly host surged out of the sky and ploughed through the ever-narrowing gap between the British and the German forces. At first glance, it looked like a cloud propelled by an invisible force. Some believed that cloud to be made up of angels.

The traditional Medieval view of angels: chubby
cherubs and severe seraphim.

Others that it was St George himself, together with the bowmen of Agincourt.

According to witnesses, this dramatic turn of events unsurprisingly sent the Germans into disarray. Their horses reared and shied, with officers battling in vain to maintain control of the startled animals. At first the Britons stared in amazement, scarcely believing their eyes. It wasn't long, however, before they realised an opportunity for escape had been heaven sent. They seized the chance and fled for their lives.

Communications were, of course, much slower in those days. It was not until May 1915 that word of this angelic apparition was circulated in the British press. The newspaper story was based on the account of a woman who had been told what occurred by two witnesses, both of them officers. In the words of the woman, the daughter of a canon in the Church of England:

'[The British soldiers]...turned round and faced the enemy, expecting nothing but instant death, when to their wonder they saw, between them and the enemy, a whole troop of angels. The German horses turned round terrified and regularly stampeded. The men tugged at their bridles while the poor beasts tore away in every direction from our men.'

There were other accounts that appeared for public consumption, including one from an officer published in the Catholic paper *The Universe*. And this one, in June 1915, from an ordinary soldier whose comrades had been faced with overwhelmingly superior enemy forces. He wrote: 'To our wonder, we saw between us an the enemy a whole troop of angels. The horses of the Germans turned round, frightened out of their senses. Evidently the horses saw the angels as clearly as we did, and the delay gave us time to reach a place of safety.'

Those who derided the soldiers' accounts usually gave as evidence for their scepticism the fact that a short story, titled 'The Bowmen', mirroring the strange incident had already been published in September 1914. In it, a soldier in a similar predicament as those at Mons cried out for the assistance of St George and the hero rode down from the sky with the bowmen in tow. Author Arthur Machen was questioned at the time as to whether there was any basis of fact in his writing. He denied it.

Yet a few weeks before Machen's story was published, Brigadier-General John Charteris had written home to tell his family: 'The angel of the Lord, on the traditional white horse, clad all in white with flaming sword, faced the advancing Germans and forbade their further progress.'

The brigadier-general could not possibly have known of Arthur Machen's fictional story. Neither could the captured German prisoners who themselves asked this question of their British captors:

'Who were your reinforcements on white horses?'

These stories, while they may have encouraged an army of hoaxers, nevertheless inspired a British public convinced that God was on their side in the 'war to end all wars'. The soldiers' families back home drank in the details and passed them on to neighbours and friends with relish, so that the story gained embellishment and momentum. In response to the demand for good news during wartime, the press was only too happy to peddle such anecdotes.

An inquiry was eventually set up by the Society for Psychical Research. Its findings appeared to put a dampener on the incident because few actual witnesses could be tracked down. Some published reports referred to a cloud appearing. Others to the arrival of St George, just as in Machen's fiction. It is clear that many of the stories of apparitions were potentially influenced by Machen's popular story. But it cannot be denied that there were other accounts – genuinely witnessed and attested by honest men – which bore remarkable similarities. So if anything did occur on the battlefields of Flanders, the genuine accounts were those that referred not to St George or Agincourt or massed bowmen...but to angels.

Angels are recognised in one form or another by almost all religions. The study of angels was developed by the ancient Persians and was absorbed into Judaism (the Hebrew *mal'akh* means 'messenger') and thence Christianity. Our word 'angel' is derived from the Greek *angelos*.

In the Bible, angels frequently intervene in human affairs, doing the Lord's work. According to Christian tradition Satan is the angel Lucifer, who was cast out of Heaven for his sins and took one-third of the Angelic Host with him to serve as demons. Those who remained continued to do God's bidding under a hierarchy of seven archangels. One medieval scholar, St Albert the Great, calculated that there were precisely 399,920,004 angels in heaven.

Angels have always been regarded as playing a role in our everyday lives. Although Protestantism largely disregarded the doctrine of angels, Catholicism generally allows each of us at least one guardian angel to protect us throughout an entire lifetime.

In recent times, the incidence of angel sightings has, if anything, increased. Nowadays, however, they are no longer chubby and child-like with feathery wings, as they were depicted in centuries gone by. They come in all shapes and forms, usually appearing as a Good Samaritan in a crisis. When they have offered their divine assistance, all traces of them mysteriously vanish.

An opinion poll in the United States in 1995 revealed that 69 per cent of people believed in the existence of angels; almost half believed they had a guardian angel; and 30 per cent claimed actually to have experienced the presence of an angel in their lives. Much as people once wore lucky heather or pixie charms, residents of 1990s America took to wearing cherub regalia in a bid to protect themselves from darker forces. They have been persuaded by the hosts of stories in circulation that angels really do exist and can help.

There have been cases of car drivers being saved from crashes and blizzards – yet afterwards there is no sign of a rescuer, no tow-truck, no tyre mark. Swimmers have been plucked from the sea just when survival seemed most remote – and afterwards discovered that the supposed lifeguard had disappeared.

Take the case of Ann Cannady, for instance. Cannady, the wife of a retired US Air Force sergeant, was suffering from uterine cancer and the prospects did not look bright. The condition was advanced and there seemed little hope left for recovery despite the gut-wrenching surgery that loomed imminently for her.

Then one day came an unexpected knock at the door of her Miami home. As the frail Cannady peered out, she was met with a bizarre sight. In front of her was a black man some 2m (6ft 6in) tall with piercing blue eyes. His words were even stranger than his appearance. He claimed his name was Thomas and that he was a messenger from

God. With that, he held up his right hand and from it came a burning white light. Before he departed, he told her that the cancer had gone. Although the incident was over in a flash, the virulent disease had, in fact, disappeared.

Some people do not even see an angel; they simply know one has been there. Like Chantal Lakey whose boyfriend tumbled to his death from a cliff overlooking the Pacific Ocean in Oregon. Chantal was trapped for hours halfway down the cliff and, despite being an agnostic, called on God to help her. 'At that moment I heard a soft choral sound,' she said. 'I was in a mist surrounded by angels – too many to count. I started falling but I remember this gigantic hand swooping down and grabbing my body. I felt the angels float me down somehow.'

Police and coastguards said afterwards that the sheer, rocky escarpment was impossible to climb up or down. They recovered Chantal and her boyfriend's body by helicopter. Of the heavenly sound that accompanied her rescue, Chantal said: 'There's nothing to describe the sound. It's like thousands of voices.'

Even more intriguing is the case of Shari Peterson, who believes that a guardian angel saved her from a horrific death on a flight from Denver, Colorado, to Auckland, New Zealand. After a stop at Honolulu, where Shari had been upgraded from a seat at the back to row 13, the Boeing 747 regained cruising altitude.

Shari was quietly reading when suddenly a voice behind her ordered her with great firmness: 'Fasten your seat belt.' She immediately looked round – but there was no one there. Nevertheless, she automatically clicked together the buckles of her belt. Less than a minute later, all hell broke loose.

A short circuit had opened the cargo door automatically and the sudden decompression tore out the side of the aircraft from rows 8 to 12. Everyone sitting in those seats had disappeared into the swirling abyss. Shari in row 13 would certainly have been sucked to her death with them but for the magical instruction to fasten her belt.

With two engines on fire, the captain could not understand how the jet stayed in the air. Miraculously, it did. And according to Shari, it was all down to a guardian angel. She said that quite apart from the supernatural warning, she also 'pictured a huge hand coming in under the aeroplane and holding it up until we landed.'

And Shari was not the only person to receive unearthly comfort on that fateful flight. Another passenger, who was desperately clinging to his wife, heard a disembodied voice tell him: 'Relax sir, you will be all right.'

CURSES

Can the doomed, the dying or even the dead summon up malicious forces with a simple curse? Are there demonic power-brokers able to bring malady and discontent, fear and even death to their opponents? The cases that follow can of course be put down to simple misfortune. But many believe that more sinister forces are at work...

Of all vessels created by man, surely none can have been as constantly cursed as the steamship *Great Eastern*. The magnificent vessel, constructed by the brilliant Victorian engineer Isambard Kingdom Brunel, was dogged by misfortune and eventually catastrophe from the day of her inception to her final watery end.

Brunel planned the *Great Eastern* to be a floating palace, intended to transport 4,000 fare-paying passengers and cargo all over the world. Work started on her in 1854. Her hull – actually two hulls, one fitting inside the other and kept apart by steel braces – was 211m (685ft) long. The double hull was divided into compartments intended to prevent a rush of water into the entire hull area if the ship was holed.

The task of constructing the hull took hundreds of men millions of hours. During its construction a riveter and his apprentice mysteriously disappeared. While the company bosses took the line that the pair had quit for other jobs, the gangers were convinced that they had been incarcerated for all time between the two hulls. With their screams drowned out in the ceaseless racket of the River Thames shipyard, their surviving workmates believed that the two unfortunates had put a foul curse upon the *Great Eastern*.

The ship was finally launched, at colossal expense, on 31 January 1858. All sorts of mishaps had befallen her while under construction because of the novel design features of this steam-powered, paddle-wheeled leviathan. But Brunel hoped that now she was in the water, she would prove her seaworthiness and her profitability.

By the time she actually hit the water, the vessel already had new owners, because her original builders had run out of money. In consequence, she was transferred from the West Indies and Australia routes, for which Brunel had intended her, to the more profitable North Atlantic crossing.

Brunel collapsed with a stroke on the day before the *Great Eastern* was to sail on her maiden voyage. He died a week later.

Shortly after his death, one of the ship's funnels exploded because a steam valve had been left closed, scalding five men to death, wrecking the ship's Grand Salon and putting the maiden voyage back indefinitely while repairs were effected. A sixth man died in one of the paddle wheels, causing further damage.

While the ship was undergoing repairs, her impatient owners ordered her towed to Holyhead, in North Wales, so that sightseers could pay to go on board and marvel at the as yet untried steamship. While there, a foul storm hit the Anglesey coast and the ship broke from her moorings. She was adrift for 18 hours and, while lesser ships might have sunk, the *Great Eastern* stayed afloat – although the salon and other rooms were again destroyed. Three months later, while still at Holyhead, the captain, coxswain and the son of another crewman drowned while out in a small boat.

The *Great Eastern* was moved from Wales back around the coast to Southampton, and it was not until 16 June 1860 that she finally left from there for New York.

The ship was under the command of a man who had never before sailed to America, and the total number of passengers was just 35. Apart from damage to the funnel casings because cheap coal was being burned to save money, there were no mishaps on the voyage west. But on an excursion trip out of New York harbour, pipes burst, flooding the accommodation areas and forcing the passengers to sleep out on deck.

Disaster once again struck the vessel on her less-than-spectacular voyage back to Britain. Near Milford Haven, South Wales, the ship became entangled in the hawser of a small boat, drowning two of its occupants. Several days later it collided with the frigate HMS *Blenheim*, causing further damage.

In 1861 and 1862, more maritime mishaps cost the owners £130,000 (a staggering sum in those days) in repair bills. It was too much for the board of the company and so, in 1864, she was sold for a mere £25,000. The vessel had never once come close to her promise of bringing wealth to her owners and luxury to her passengers.

The *Great Eastern* then embarked on the one and only profitable exercise she had undertaken: laying telegraph cables across the Atlantic Ocean and in the tropics from Bombay to Aden. But in the 1870s, with the advent of ships specifically designed for the task, she was obsolete even for this purpose. Following a further collision, off the River Mersey's estuary, she was broken up for scrap in 1886.

Men who had devoted their lives to the sea could never recall a vessel dogged with so much ill luck. Perhaps the answer lay in the ship's unique double hull.

When demolition experts ripped open the steel plating, they found the bodies of the riveter and his apprentice – their skeletal remains fixed in a pose of grisly desperation as they had tried to claw their way through the impenetrable hull.

There is no doubt that the *Great Eastern* was jinxed. But was it cursed? If a jinx is the unexplained bringer of bad luck, a curse is the conscious wish of someone to bring down upon an enemy ill fortune, ill health or even worse.

One man who knew without doubt that he was doomed by virtue of a curse was archaeologist Professor Stephen Resden. He opened the tomb of the pharaoh Sennar in the 1890s and read an inscription: 'Whoever desecrates the tomb of King Sennar will be overtaken by the sands and destroyed.' A strong believer in the powers of the occult, Resden knew his days were numbered. Aboard ship on his voyage home to Europe, the professor inexplicably died of suffocation. The ship's doctor found that in his hands were clutched small amounts of sand.

More notorious still than the curses of the pharaohs are voodoo curses. Fuller examples of the power of both are revealed in other chapters in this volume (The Curse of Tutankhamun on page 47 and Voodoo on page 19). However, here is one brief example of a voodoo curse that killed...

In the early 1960s Robert Heinl served as a US Marine Corps colonel in Haiti and became deeply interested in the voodoo religion, the black art practised by the natives. After returning to the United

States, Heinl penned a book, *Written in Blood*, which criticised the atmosphere in which voodoo flourished: namely, the despotic regime of Papa Doc Duvalier and his Tontons Macoutes, the armed sentinels of his brutal, totalitarian regime.

In 1971, after the tyrant's death, his widow Simone placed a curse upon Heinl and his yet unpublished book. Strange things began to happen. His book was lost on the way to the publisher; then the manuscript was found four months later in a deserted room which the publisher said was never used. A reporter assigned to interview Heinl nearly died of appendicitis, and Heinl himself was badly bitten by a dog and hospitalised.

Robert Heinl finally died, in torment, of a heart attack on the Caribbean island of St Barthelemy in May 1979. He had scoffed at the voodoo belief that the power of the curse becomes stronger the nearer the victim is to Haiti.

In 1980 a strange Aboriginal curse was reinvoked in the Australian Outback when a boulder was removed from a religious site. The boulder formed part of the so-called Devil's Marbles, which the Aborigines said had been cursed by their forefathers from time immemorial.

When the boulder was removed to a national park, Aboriginal leader Mick Taylor warned that sickness and death would follow. Several Aboriginal children fell ill and Taylor himself caught meningitis. An urgent meeting of councillors in the town of Tennant Creek had the stone returned and the children completely recovered. But it was too late for poor Mick Taylor.

An exquisite gem, the priceless Hope Diamond, was cursed by a woman who blamed it for her marital unhappiness. Hewn from the mines of Golcond, in southern India, the diamond originally belonged to Louis XIV of France and disappeared during the French Revolution. It was bought in 1830 by a wealthy diamond collector, Henry Hope, who escaped ill fortune. But he handed it on to his cousin, Lord Francis Hope, whose wife laid the curse on it. Because she blamed the failure of the miserable marriage upon the stone, she prophesied evil for all its future owners.

A French diamond dealer, Jacques Colot, purchased the Hope Diamond in 1904 and sold it at a handsome profit to a Russian nobleman, Prince Kanitovski. Colot went mad and committed suicide within months of concluding the deal. Shortly afterwards, at the Folies Bergères in Paris, Prince Kanitovski shot and killed an actress to whom he had loaned the diamond. He was killed himself by a radical mob just days later.

A Greek jeweller who acquired the stone was next to die, falling into a ravine. In 1908 ownership passed to the sultan of Turkey, Abdul Hamid II, who was overthrown in 1909. The next man to acquire the stone drowned in November of the same year. The last private owner was newspaper magnate Edward McLean, whose child died in a car crash before he himself became an alcoholic and was driven mad.

The jewel then passed from him to Washington's Smithsonian Institute where, safe behind bulletproof glass, it has brought no harm to anyone.

THE CURSE OF
TUTANKHAMUN

O f the original team of archaeologists who were present when the ancient tomb of the boy king Tutankhamun was opened, only one lived to a ripe old age. Was this a bizarre coincidence? Or was it the manifestation of a curse that had passed down through the centuries – a curse too sinister, too mysterious and too lethal for the modern world to comprehend? And a curse that is still exacting its deadly toll today...

The final wall of the sealed burial chamber of the boy pharaoh was breached for the first time in 3,000 years on 17 February 1923. Archaeologist Howard Carter whispered breathlessly that he could see 'things, wonderful things' as he gazed in awe at the treasures of Tutankhamun.

As Carter, together with fanatical Egyptologist Lord Carnarvon, looked at the treasures of gold, gems, precious stones and other priceless relics, they ignored the dire warning written all those centuries ago to ward off grave robbers. In the ancient hieroglyphics above their heads, it read: 'Death will come to those who disturb the sleep of the pharaohs.'

The final blow of the excavators' pick had set free the Curse of the Pharaoh.

Lord Carnarvon had never taken lightly the threats of ancient Egypt's high priests. In England before his expedition had set out, he had consulted a famous mystic of the day, Count Hamon, who warned him: 'Lord Carnarvon not to enter tomb. Disobey at peril. If ignored will suffer sickness. Not recover. Death will claim him in Egypt.' Two separate visits to mediums in England had also prophesied his impending doom.

But for Carter and Lord Carnarvon, who had financed the dig culminating in history's greatest archaeological find, all thoughts of curses and hocus-pocus were forgotten as they revelled in the joy of the victorious end to the dig.

The site of Luxor had escaped the attentions of grave robbers down through the centuries, and the treasure-packed tomb was a find beyond compare. The accolades of the world's academics rained down on him and his team. The praise of museums and seats of learning as far apart as Cairo and California was heaped on them. Carnarvon revelled in the glittering prize of fame – little knowing that he had but two months to enjoy the fruits of his success.

On 5 April 1923, just 47 days after breaching the chamber into Tutankhamun's resting place, Carnarvon, aged 57, died in agony – the victim, apparently, of an infected mosquito bite.

At the moment of his death in the Continental Hotel, Cairo, the lights in the city went out in unison, and stayed off for some minutes. And if further proof were needed that it was indeed a strange force that was at work, thousands of miles away in England, at Lord Carnarvon's country house, his dog began baying and howling – a blood-curdling, unnatural lament which shocked the domestic staff deep in the middle of the night. It continued until one last whine, when the tormented creature turned over and died.

The newspapers of the day were quick to speculate that such eerie happenings were caused by the curse, an untapped source of evil which Carnarvon and Carter had unleashed. Their sensational conclusion was reinforced when, two days after Carnarvon's death, the mummified body of the pharaoh was examined and a blemish was found on his left cheek exactly in the position of the mosquito bite on Carnarvon's face.

Perhaps this could have been passed off as coincidence had it not been for the bizarre chain of deaths that were to follow.

Shortly after Carnarvon's demise, another archaeologist, Arthur Mace, a leading member of the expedition, went into a coma at the Hotel Continental after complaining of tiredness. He died soon afterwards, leaving the expedition medic and local doctors baffled.

The deaths continued. A close friend of Carnarvon, George Gould, made the voyage to

Egypt when he learned of his fate. Before leaving the port to travel to Cairo he looked in at the tomb. The following day he collapsed with a high fever; twelve hours later he was dead.

Radiologist Archibald Reid, a man who used the latest X-ray techniques to determine the age and possible cause of death of Tutankhamun, was sent back to England after complaining of exhaustion. He died soon after landing.

Carnarvon's personal secretary, Richard Bethell, was found dead in bed from heart failure four months after the discovery of the tomb.

The casualties continued to mount. Joel Wool, a leading British industrialist of the time, visited the site and was dead a few months later from a fever which doctors could not comprehend.

Six years after the discovery, 12 of those present when the tomb was opened were dead. Within a further seven years only two of the original team of excavators were still alive. Lord Carnarvon's half-brother apparently took his own life while temporarily insane, and a further 21 people connected in some way with the dig, were also dead. Of the original pioneers of the excavation, only Howard Carter lived to a ripe old age, dying in 1939 from natural causes.

Others have not been so fortunate. While countless Egyptologists and academics have tried to debunk the legend of the curse as pure myth, others have continued to fall victim to its influence...

Mohammed Ibrahim, Egypt's director of antiquities, in 1966 argued with the government against letting the treasures from the tomb leave Egypt for an exhibition in Paris. He pleaded with the authorities to allow the relics to stay in Cairo because he had suffered terrible nightmares of what would happen to him if they left the country. Ibrahim left a final meeting with the government officials, stepped out into what looked like a clear road on a bright sunny day, was hit by a car and died instantly.

Perhaps even more bizarre was the case of Richard Adamson who by 1969 was the sole surviving member of the 1923 expedition. Adamson had lost his wife within 24 hours of speaking out against the curse. His son broke his back in an aircraft crash when he spoke out again.

Still sceptical, Adamson, who had worked as a security guard for Lord Carnarvon, defied the curse and gave an interview on British television, in which he still said that he did not believe in the curse. Later that evening, as he left the television studios, he was thrown from his taxi when it crashed, a swerving lorry missed his head by inches, and he was put in hospital with fractures and bruises. It was only then that the stoic Mr Adamson, then aged 70, was forced to admit: 'Until now I refused to believe that my family's misfortunes had anything to do with the curse. But now I am not so sure.'

Perhaps the most amazing manifestation of the curse came in 1972, when the treasures of the tomb were transported to London for a prestigious exhibition at the British Museum. Victim number one was Dr Gamal Mehrez, Ibrahim's successor in Cairo as director of antiquities. He scoffed at the legend, saying that his whole life had been spent in Egyptology and that all the deaths and misfortune through the decades had been the result of 'pure coincidence'. He died the night after supervising the packaging of the relics for transport to England by a Royal Air Force plane.

The crew members of that aircraft suffered death, injury, misfortune and disaster in the years that followed their cursed flight.

Flight Lieutenant Rick Laurie died in 1976 from a heart attack. His wife declared: 'It's the curse of Tutankhamun – the curse has killed him.'

Ken Parkinson, a flight engineer, suffered a heart attack each year at the same time as the flight aboard the Britannia aircraft which brought the treasures to England until a final fatal one in 1978. Before their mission to Egypt neither of the servicemen had suffered any heart trouble, and had been pronounced fit by military doctors.

During the flight, Chief Technical Officer Ian Lansdown kicked the crate that contained the death mask of the boy king. 'I've just kicked the most expensive thing in the world,' he quipped. Later, on disembarking from the aircraft on another mission, a ladder mysteriously broke beneath him and the leg he had kicked the crate with was badly broken. It was in plaster for nearly six months.

Flight Lieutenant Jim Webb, who was aboard the aircraft, lost everything he owned after a fire devastated his home. A steward, Brian Rounsfall, confessed to playing cards on the sarcophagus of Tutankhamun on the flight home and suffered two heart attacks. And a woman officer on board the plane was forced to leave the RAF after having a serious operation.

The mystery remains. Were all those poor souls down the years merely the victims of some gigantic set of coincidences? Or did the priestly guardians of the tomb's dark secrets really exert supernatural forces which heaped so much misery and suffering on those who invaded their sacred chambers – and exact a terrible punishment on the despoilers of the magnificent graves of their noble dead?

The most intriguing theory to explain the legend of the curse was advanced by atomic scientist Louis Bulgarini in 1949. He wrote:

'It is definitely possible that the ancient Egyptians use atomic radiation to protect their holy places. The floors of the tombs could have been covered with uranium. Or the graves could have been finished with radioactive rock. Rock containing both gold and uranium was mined in Egypt. Such radiation could kill a man today.'

CHRIST'S RELICS

The parish priest was intent on improving his little church. His was a poor community and there was little money for the necessities of life, never mind paint, plaster and ornaments. The priest, Abbé Berenger Sauniere, knew that whatever renovations needed to be done, he would have to do himself. The penniless priest set about his task in the summer of 1891.

One of the first things the Abbé did was to remove an altar stone that lay across two broad columns. One of them, he discovered, was hollow and inside were four tubes containing parchments. Some were in code and to this day no one knows what was written on the documents. But they set the priest on a fabulous trail, an odyssey of mystery and adventure – a journey to a secret source of wealth.

Suddenly his Church of St Magdalene became filled with glittering ornaments and Rennes-le-Chateau, the village in which it nestles, became wealthy beyond the wildest dreams of its farm-worker inhabitants. The priest's pay was £6 a year. Yet he spent an astonishing £10 million on his church, on the village, on missionary work – and on himself.

Father Berenger built a modern road up to the village. He piped in water. He hired craftsmen from all over Europe to redecorate the church in a lurid fashion, with hideous statues and gaudy plaques. He constructed a lavish villa for himself and his housekeeper, with a splendid wood-panelled study in a tower overlooking decorative gardens containing a pretty orangery. He filled the villa with a collection of rare china, precious fabrics, antique marble and a magnificent library. He threw regular banquets for his parishioners and he gave cash handouts to the locals. He financed missionary work in Africa and he funded convents and monasteries.

Today the church and the villa still stand in the hamlet of Rennes-le-Chateau, huddled on the foothills of the Pyrenees in southern France. It is a tightly knit community of farm workers and grape pickers living in neat white cottages. The thin mountain air is filled with the swish of scythes and the call of birds. Only the occasional visitor comes to investigate one of the most tantalising mysteries of all time.

What wonderful – or dreadful – secret did Father Berenger Sauniere uncover in his church a century and more before? Was it a hidden horde of plundered treasure? Was it the Holy Grail, the cup Christ drank from at the Last Supper? Or was it a secret so terrible that the Pope himself paid a fortune to keep it hidden forever?

Father Berenger never revealed where the village's sudden wealth came from. And the only person to share his secret, his housekeeper Marie, kept her silence to the grave.

The only clues to the mystery of Rennes-le-Chateau are the constant flow of important guests, from Catholic Church officials to politicians, who visited the village after the priest's discovery. One of his most frequent visitors was the Archduke Johann von Habsburg, a cousin of the emperor of Austria-Hungary. It was subsequently found that Habsburg and Sauniere had opened consecutively numbered bank accounts and that considerable sums of money had been transferred to the priest. In addition, this simple country priest had no fewer than seven bulging accounts in other banks across Europe.

Sauniere refused to accept either promotion or a transfer, and an attempt to have him thrown out of the church for illegally selling Masses was overruled by the Pope. In 1917, as Sauniere lay dying, a priest was called to hear his final confession – and was so shocked by what Sauniere told him that he refused to give him absolution.

Not even Sauniere's will threw any light on the mystery, for it showed him to be penniless. He had switched his wealth to his housekeeper Marie, who continued to live in comfort at the villa until 1946. In that year, the French government issued a new currency and, before the banks would exchange new francs for old, everyone was obliged to decla. exactly how they had obtained their money. Marie did not – and was seen in her garden burning bundles of the useless old notes. She chose to live in poverty rather than reveal her secret.

Eventually Marie sold the villa so that she could live on the proceeds of the transaction. She promised the new owner, Noel Corbu, that she would tell him her secret before she died. But in 1953 she suffered a stroke which left her incapable of speech and she died unable or unwilling to communicate the answer to the puzzle.

So how was it that Berenger Sauniere, who earned only £6 a year as a parish priest, was able to spend the fabulous sum of £10 million in 25 years?

The most extraordinary but most widely circulated theory of all is that the priest discovered that Christ's crucifixion was an elaborate subterfuge and that the Catholic Church bought his silence. Several books have been written about this controversial theory. In them, it is supposed that the altar documents Sauniere discovered traced the family tree of an old French royal dynasty – establishing direct descent from Christ.

It is claimed that, contrary to Christian belief, Jesus was married to Mary Magdalene and they had children who married into European royalty. Far from being a poor carpenter, so the theory goes,

Jesus was in reality an aristocrat and his miracles simply magician's tricks. His crucifixion, ordered by the Romans who were worried about his popularity, was faked. After sniffing opium on the cross, he was unconscious and appeared to be dead. This allowed him to 'rise from the dead' after being placed in the tomb.

Christ supposedly lived on in the Holy Land for another 40 years. But Mary, their children and several relatives took a ship to France. They landed in Marseilles and eventually settled in Rennes-le-Chateau. There the children met and married into the French nobility, principally the Merovingian dynasty which was based around Rennes.

Sauniere, it has been suggested, showed the newly discovered family tree to the wealthy descendants almost 2,000 years later. They paid him millions to find out more and to keep his mouth shut until they could claim their lineage unchallenged. The Vatican, however, countered by giving the priest money rather than allow the Bible story to be questioned.

This theory has been developed further by some researchers into the priest's secret. They claim that Christ's body was actually brought to France and buried, along with his family treasure and documentary evidence, beneath the so-called Eternal Spring in the nearby area known as Le Valdieu – the Vale of God. This peaceful valley is three miles from

Rennes-le-Chateau and it is believed that the two places are linked by secret tunnels. The priest and his housekeeper used to go for long walks in the countryside and would return lugging heavy bags.

The Vale of God hides a secret even older than Father Berenger's mysterious discovery of 1891. A trail of ciphers and clues has led historians to a spring which pours from the earth there. The so-called Eternal Spring covered over by an arched wall when the water was diverted some 200 years ago. This was thought to have been the burial site of sacred relics or gold, brought to the area by the Visigoths, one of the Teutonic tribes that plundered the wealth of the Roman Empire.

In the 1960s an Englishwoman, Celia Brooke, came to Rennes and took on the task of looking after St Mary Magdalene Church. She raises new questions about the priests' wealth:

'Behind the altar there is a room where Sauniere used to lock himself away after services. No one would ever see Sauniere leave it yet he would be spotted later on carrying heavy sacks. We have found a hidden passageway out of the church from this room. I believe he used it to make his way down to the Vale of God, probably by tunnel. But I have been here a quarter of a century and I still don't know the answer to the mystery. I don't think we ever will.'

Another Englishwoman, Patricia Logan, who

settled in the Vale of God in 1982, discovered that her land enclosed the site of the original spring. At the time she moved to France from her home town of York, she had no idea of the stories that one of the world's most mystifying fortunes could be buried in or around her back garden. Patricia, who runs a guest house in the valley, says:

'The legends talk of a man-made pool which hides an amazing treasure, and there is man-made pool here. There have been all sorts of theories about what was hidden beneath it. Some people believe that it is treasure taken from the temple of Jerusalem thousands of years ago. Others think that it could be the Holy Grail from which Christ drank at the Last Supper and which was used to catch drops of his blood at the Crucifixion. Others even think the "riches" are the remains of Christ himself.

'I can't wait for the wall to crumble so I can dig beneath the foundations but I won't let bulldozers spoil the countryside. It is very strange to think that sometimes I might be standing on Christ's tomb. If this is his last resting place, it would make the priest's supposed grave robbery all the more horrifying. It could explain why he was refused the last rites.'

Antoine Captier keeps Sauniere's correspondence and papers to this day. He thinks the key to the mystery might lie in a secret crypt deep beneath the church.

Captier, a descendant of the priest's bell-ringer, says:

'In his diary of 21 September 1891 the Abbé refers to "the discovery of a tomb". This might refer to a crypt beneath the church but no one has found it since. It has been said that the crypt contains tombstones which resemble those of the Merovingian kings – the French royal line supposed to descend from Christ. That might explain theories about a blood line stretching to the present day.'

Antoine Captier believes the most likely explanation for the old priest's wealth is that he found some gold but supplemented it by selling Masses. Of the fake crucifixion theory, Captier says:

'Why should Christ's apparent descendants want to keep such a proud claim quiet? Why wouldn't they investigate it themselves rather than leave it to Sauniere, a parish priest with no apparent resources? Why should the Vatican accept that the family tree was anything but a medieval forgery? And why should so many important people allow themselves to be blackmailed by a simple country priest? Despite all the books written about Rennes-le-Chateau, no one has ever proved any of these theories.

'I have grown up with this mystery. One day the answer will come out but only when the time is right. And that time is not now.'

One possible explanation for the merging of

two mysteries about the hidden wealth of Rennes-le-Chateau and the Vale of God is that references to the Holy Grail are really a corruption of the French words *Sang Real,* meaning the royal blood. Was this, after all, what Father Berenger Sauniere discovered? That Christ's descendants came to France almost two millennia ago – and may, unknowingly, still be living in the region to this day?

None of these theories, however, explains why Sauniere's deathbed confession was so horrifying that he was refused the last rites. Local farmer François Sauzede has the last word. Tapping his stick on the sunbaked soil, he says:

'I have known since I was a child that the key to power, riches and fame is buried here. That is the knowledge that my father and grandfather gave me. Everyone else in the village was brought up knowing it too. But just try finding out where or even what the secret is.'

THE TURIN SHROUD

The most awesome of all Christian relics lies in three padlocked containers behind secure iron grilles in a north Italian cathedral. It is the Shroud of Turin, which many still believe was the linen cloth wrapped around the body of Christ when he was laid in the tomb.

The flaxen shroud, 4.3m (14ft) long and 3.1m (3ft 6in) wide, has been treated as a serious relic for 'only' about a century. Claims have always been made for it that it had once contained Christ's remains – but the same claims had been made for almost 50 other shrouds in churches throughout Europe.

It was only when Secundo Pia, an Italian archaeologist and amateur photographer, took the first ever picture of the shroud in the Chapel of the Dukes at Turin Cathedral in 1898 that its significance began to be realised. For when Pia's negative was studied, it seemed to produce the face of Christ.

Nevertheless, it was not until 1931 that a proper scientific investigation was allowed. This time a professional cameraman, Guiseppe Enri, carefully captured the image on the shroud in a lengthy photographic study. Suddenly the Shroud of Turin was world famous, and many of the sceptics

The face of Christ or a clever medieval fake? The
Shroud of Turin still holds its secrets.

were instantly converted. The man is naked, 1.8m (5ft 11in) tall. He is bearded, with long hair hanging down his back and at shoulder-length at the sides. His hands are modestly crossed over his loins. There are indications that he has been tortured and crucified; the hands had probably been nailed through the palms and the feet had been fastened by a single nail. The sole of one foot appears to be darkened with blood.

The man's side had been pierced, presumably with a spear, and there is the possibility that patterns across the body could have been caused by up to a hundred lashes, which in those days would have been inflicted with a scourge – a flail with metal balls attached.

The hair is matted with blood. Blood has also coagulated in scratches on the forehead. Was this the result of the crown of thorns placed upon the head of Christ to mock the 'King of the Jews'?

If this was the winding sheet of Christ, how did it get to Turin? First mention of a burial shroud comes in the Gospel of St Mark, traditionally dated to AD 65, which talks of the cloth in which Christ was wrapped being found in his empty tomb. Pilgrims to Jerusalem, writing 300 years later, mention seeing a holy shroud.

The next recorded appearance of a relic purporting to be Christ's burial shroud is in Constantinople (now Istanbul), from which it was taken in the 13th century and moved to France. The Shroud of Turin makes its first definite appearance in the 15th century, in a silver casket in Sainte Chapelle, at Chambéry, specially built by Louis I, duke of Savoy, to house the relic. It was damaged in 1532, however, when a fire partly destroyed the chapel, and this is believed to be the cause of two symmetrical scorch marks on the fabric.

It is assumed that the cloth was rescued from the fire and was repaired by nuns. In 1572 the present shroud was transported to Turin Cathedral, where it remained under the ownership of the dukes of Savoy ever since. In the 19th century the Vatican seemed to play down the importance of the shroud, issuing a proclamation that even if it 'be the most sacred [relic] in Christendom', they could not guarantee its authenticity.

Perhaps as a result of the Vatican's own disquiet, public showings of the Turin Shroud have been extremely rare – only three times this century. In 1978 it was on display for all of 42 days, during which more than three million pilgrims filed past. There was little they could discern, however, for the image of a crucified man can only been seen through the photographed image.

So how did the image come to be imprinted so indelibly that it miraculously survived 2,000 years of primitive storage? For, in most senses, a miracle it seems to be.

Blood alone would not have dyed the shroud with such a precise image. Chemists have postulated that ammonia from the skin, in sweat and as a gas, could have stained the linen. Another suggested source is Jewish ritual burial spices.

Less scientific sounding was the theory that the Resurrection caused a supernatural release of energy which scorched the fabric. However, this theory got backing from the US Air Force – whose scientists said that the marks on the shroud appeared to have been caused by a micro-second blast of intense radiation.

Then came evidence which cast huge doubts about the antiquity of the shroud. In 1988 three separate laboratories conducted carbon dating experiments on centimetre-square samples of cloth supplied by the Vatican – and declared categorically that it was no older than the 14th century. This was about the time that the relic turned up mysteriously in a small French village.

Additional scorn was poured upon the miracle in 1994 by researchers Lynn Picknett and Clive Prince who wrote a book, *Turin Shroud*, proclaiming that the relic was an extraordinarily elaborate hoax, perpetrated by a genius. That man, they said, was none other than Leonardo da Vinci, the most inventive scientist and artist who ever lived. Why should he perpetrate such a hoax? On the orders of Pope Innocent VIII, who needed a fresh religious relic to boost his popularity.

To counter the scepticism, however, have come two significantly fresh appraisals. German researchers Elmar Gruber and Holger Kersten, who wrote a book *The Jesus Conspiracy*, believe that 'the carbon dating by the laboratories was impeccable but the samples they dated do not stem from the shroud'. The samples of flax, prepared under unexplained secrecy, were switched by the Vatican. The reasoning was that, since the winding sheet had been around a dead man, any evidence that it was a genuine relic would also have proved that Christ had lain dead long enough to cause such an imprint. 'That would have destroyed the entire story of the Resurrection,' said Gruber.

Strong backing for the veracity of the shroud came from Cambridge-educated scientist Rodney Hoare, who spent 26 years researching the relic and who wrote a book titled *The Turin Shroud Is Genuine*. He argued that the carbon-dating laboratories were bound to get it wrong because – unlike most objects they analyse, the shroud had been constantly exposed and handled for almost 2,000 years. Fingerprints, fire, pollutants and other factors, such as the high carbon content in treated flax, made nonsense of the carbon dating figures.

Hoare, who became chairman of the British Society for the Turin Shroud, concludes that the relic is no fake. It could not have been created by a paintbrush – 'because it is a negative image that holds three-dimensional information of a nature that no artist could produce'.

After all, how could a mediaeval artist have produced a negative image? No one knew what one was until the invention of photography!

Hoare is also certain that the body that was once wrapped in the Turin Shroud was alive. The markings are evenly distributed, showing that there was no rigor mortis. The man was therefore taken from the Cross in a coma on the Friday evening. The burial was then interrupted by the Jewish sabbath. On Sunday they would have discovered that the body was still warm and would have spirited away the survivor to recover in secret.

Was the person wrapped in the Turin Shroud indeed Jesus? Rodney Hoare says: 'We can tell that the man had been nailed through his wrists and feet. He had been scourged and his chest pierced with a spear. Small wounds on the head indicate the crown of thorns.' Comparing this evidence with the Gospels, Hoare adds: 'The lancing of the chest is reported in only two other contemporary cases. And the crown of thorns was unique to Jesus.'

If Rodney Hoare is right, the Turin Shroud was wrapped around the body of Christ – a miraculous example of the ultimate supernatural power.

STIGMATA AND WEEPING IMAGES

It was Gemma Galgani's lifelong dream to become a nun. Instead, crippled by spinal tuberculosis, she was compelled to live the simple life of a peasant girl in turn-of-the-century Italy. One event, however, was destined to change the 23-year-old orphan girl's life and identify her with the suffering of Jesus Christ far more tellingly than any sister in the Passionist Order that had spurned her.

It was a warm Friday in March 1901 when Gemma went through her daily supplications before a large crucifix in the village where she lived. There was nothing unusual, such was Gemma's devotion to her faith. It was only later, when her foster mother entered the room, that Gemma's case became the talk of Italy.

Gemma was found with whip-like marks on her back, and her clothes were soaked with blood. From then to her death, two years later, the girl exhibited stigmata with unerring regularity each Thursday. The marks of Christ would have faded by the following day and by Sunday would have left only faint traces.

Father Germano di Stanislao, Gemma's biographer, described how the wound developed, reddening slowly on the back and palm of her hands. They were, he said, very deep, apparently passing right through the hand itself they were also full of blood, some of it flowing. Years after her death, Gemma was beatified and became a saint, as much for her devotion to her faith as for the astonishing stigmata that brought her fame.

Stigmata – replicas of the physical wounds suffered by Christ during the crucifixion – are a phenomenon constantly recurring, even today. Probably the best known stigmatic was St Francis of Assisi who, after prayer one day in 1224, found his hands and feet pierced by nails, causing so much pain he could not walk.

Critical historians claim the story of St Francis's stigmata was an invention to further his fame. Medical evidence, based on people who displayed similar signs, suggests the saint, renowned for his care of animals, was indeed a stigmatic.

A rare 20th century case of a male stigmatic was that of Padre Pio Forgione, a Capuchin friar whom the phenomenon affected from the age of 28, in 1915. A humble, self-effacing man, he tried to hide the horrible hand wounds that afflicted him and rarely appeared in public. Doctors attested to his stigmata, saying that the priest's palms were permanently pierced right through.

Padre Pio died in the monastery at Foggia,

Italy, where he had regularly passed into a state of ecstasy while saying mass – and where a cupful of blood would flow from his wounds each day.

A more recent case miraculously occurred in 1926. On Good Friday of that year, a blind and paralysed 20-year-old German girl, Teresa Neumann, experienced a vision of her namesake, St Therese of Lisieux, and was cured of her afflictions as suddenly as they had first struck her down six years earlier.

However, every Friday for the next 36 years until her death in 1962, Teresa suffered the marks of stigmata. For 24 hours she would fall into a trance and exhibit deep, rectangular wounds to her hands, which healed as swiftly as they appeared. Witnesses even described her shedding tearlets of blood from her feet, her side and her forehead.

As part of her devotions, Teresa ate only communion wafers and wine. But this humble and hallowed diet sustained her through continued periods of stigmata, ecstasies and visions.

Most people suffering stigmata tend to shun the spotlight and hide their grisly injuries. One who didn't was Clemente Dominguez, a Spanish mystic whose stigmata manifested itself in a 'crown of thorns' injury, making blood flow from his forehead. During the 1970s, Clemente positively revelled in his fame and his many followers believed him to be a saint.

While most Roman Catholic theologians accept many of the stories of stigmata as being genuine, doctors explain away the phenomenon as being caused by the effects of a subdued form of hysteria, with wounds differing according to how they imagine Christ was crucified.

Strangely, there are no known examples of stigmata sufferers exhibiting wounds around the wrists – where researchers of the Turin Shroud suggest they should be.

One of the most extensive investigations into stigmatism was undertaken by Dr Imbert Gourbeyre in 1984. He researched a total of 321 cases and since only 41 were male, concluded that the phenomenon was far more likely to affect pious or fervently religious women. A survey conducted in 1936 by Father Herbert Thurston seemed to show that cases of stigmata were on the increase – and, again, almost exclusively affected women.

Can inanimate objects, such as statues, icons, paintings or photographs, actually to bleed or weep? The phenomena of weeping Madonnas – holy images that appear to shed tears – have long been castigated as trickery by sceptics. Yet in many cases, scientists can provide no credible explanations, other than the power of faith.

Just after Easter 1975, Mrs Anne Pore was praying before before a metre-high plastic statuette of Jesus at her home in Boothwyn, Pennsylvania, when she noticed two drops of ruby red blood ooz-ing from the figure's palms. A devout Catholic, Mrs Poore was moved to build a shrine for the statue in her porch, and each Friday and on holy days it poured forth a tiny stream of blood.

And blood it was. A respected Philadelphia physician, Dr Joseph Rovito, conducted a thorough examination of the statuette, using X-rays in an attempt to uncover its inner secrets. He concluded that there was no in-built trick mechanism. Additionally, the doctor found the blood tests strangely macabre; although it was undeniably human blood, the low red cell count indicated that it was of great age. And he was unable to determine its blood type.

In May 1994 a retired Irish postmistress, 78-year-old Mary Murray, saw tears fall from a statue in her house at Grangecon, County Wicklow. Visitors queued up to witness the bloodied teardrops which fell from the eyes of the plaster model. Its makers, a Portuguese company, said that the glass eyes were held in place with wax, glue and other substances which could possibly have melted if exposed to high temperatures.

Learned medical opinion also testified that blood wept by a 300-year-old wooden crucifix of Christ in the church of Porta das Caixa, Brazil, was human. The site became a shrine renowned for its miraculous cures.

An Italian doctor, Piero Casoli, undertook an exhaustive study of weeping Madonnas and discovered that the phenomena occurred as often as twice a year in Italy alone. Once natural causes, including chicanery, had been ruled out, he concluded that liquid appearing on the surfaces of such statues was derived from a mysterious source. His only explanation was 'teleportation'. Dr Casoli also noted such events were no accident; they all occurred at centres of religious devotions.

One of the most celebrated cases of a weeping Madonna was in Syracuse, Sicily, where newlywed Antoinetta Janusso fell ill with a malaise that puzzled local medics. After suffering fits and convulsions, interspersed with periods of blindness and deafness, Antoinetta lay sick in her room. One day she noticed a statuette of the Virgin Mary above her bed begin to shed tears. Within hours, she felt well enough to get up, and her mysterious illness disappeared altogether.

The statue continued to weep for almost a week, and reliable witnesses – apart from Antoinetta, who feared she would be accused of hysteria – testified to the miracle.

JOHN BRADBURNE

The outward manifestations of life after death can create in witnesses either of two extreme emotions. In some cases, as we have seen from many of the stories in this book, the reaction is sheer terror. In other cases, however, the emotions are quite the opposite. In the case of John Bradburne, not only did his influence extend beyond the grave, the mysterious circumstances of his passing caused him to be beatified by the people among whom he had lived.

Bradburne was an Englishman who worked selflessly with lepers in the poor, rural areas of Zimbabwe. It cost him his home, his freedom and eventually his life. Yet the manner of his death and the mysterious circumstances of his funeral have created a legend. Many who were there that day are convinced they witnessed a miracle. To them, the name of John Bradburne is synonymous with sainthood.

Bradburne was the son of a Norfolk country parson. He saw service as a Gurkha officer during the Second World War and after the fall of Singapore was forced into the Malayan jungle, an ordeal he survived through a combination of luck and quick wits. He emerged from the war mentally scarred by some of the horrors he had seen but also with the lifelong friendship of a fellow officer, John Dove, later a Jesuit priest.

Back in civvie street, Bradburne drifted into a few jobs, including forestry and teaching. His powerful faith combined with a growing restlessness eventually drove him into the arms of the church and he converted to Roman Catholicism in 1947. He flirted with becoming a monk, made a pilgrimage to Jerusalem and, while living in Southern Italy, made a commitment to celibacy in his prayers to the Virgin Mary. Those who knew the likable, good-looking, well-spoken Englishman believed that he was desperately seeking an outlet for his faith, a life-mission to carry out God's work.

He found it shortly before his 40th birthday when John Dove, by now a priest in Rhodesia (as it was then known), invited him to come for a visit. Even then, Bradburne seemed unable to settle. It wasn't until 1969, when his friend Heather Benoy suggested they visit a leper camp at Mutemwa, that his future path became clear. He refused to return home to Salisbury (now Harare) and became the warden of this filthy shambles of a settlement. He was to spend the rest of his life there.

Over the next 10 years, Bradburne introduced standards of care and hygiene that his crippled patients had never dreamed of. He cleared the rats that would gnaw their senseless limbs at night, cut the nails of those who still had fingers and toes and fed and bathed them. He wrote poems about each of the 80 cripples under his care, and when any were close to death he gave them inspirational strength by reading to them from the Bible. He also supervised the building of a small chapel in the settlement.

In time, Bradburne fell out with members of the Rhodesia Leprosy Association. They objected to his 'extravagance' at demanding one loaf of bread per leper per week. And they were appalled when he refused to place numbers around the necks of the lepers. 'These are men, not livestock,' he would say.

Bradburne was expelled from the settlement, though he refused to leave the area. He lived in a tin hut on a nearby mountain, often ministering to his patients under cover of the night. With his long hair and beard, monk's habit (he had been granted the habit of a Third Order Franciscan) and emaciated figure, he was instantly recognisable.

By the summer of 1979, the civil war in Rhodesia was at its height. Main roads were kept open by the government but in much of the countryside Patriotic Front guerrillas were in the ascendancy. The colony at Mutemwa fell well within their sphere of influence.

At midnight on 2 September, a group of 10 Mujibha youths – the messengers and intelligence gathers of Robert Mugabe's army – called at

Bradburne's hut and kidnapped him. His friends suspected that he had been falsely denounced as a Rhodesian spy by a worker at Mutemwa, whom Bradburne had reprimanded for stealing rations reserved for lepers. Bradburne was taken to a meeting of hundreds of teenage Mujibhas who mocked and abused him. They offered him excrement to eat, tried to make him dance to their music and offered him local girls to sleep with.

The following day the professional guerrillas took over and led Bradburne to a cave near the settlement of Gwaze. They were furious with the Mujibhas for taking him away from Mutemwa because their information was that he was a good man. But they were also worried about returning him. They feared he might give information on their hideout to the authorities.

During his interrogation, the Englishman seemed oblivious to the questioning. At one point he knelt and prayed for 10 minutes, infuriating the rebel commander. He rejected most of their food and when they suggested he could go and live in a neutral country like China (Mugabe's chief provider of aid), he laughed out loud. Similarly he rejected an offer to work in Mozambique. 'I must return to the lepers at Mutemwa,' he told them.

That night Bradburne was marched towards the nearest main road where the guerrilla commander ordered him to walk a few paces ahead. He was then told to turn and face the commander but he fell on his knees and prayed, showing not a flicker of fear. When he rose to his feet the commander shot him.

The body was found the following morning by the only other white man still in the area, a Roman Catholic priest called Father David Gibbs. Gibbs knew Bradburne well. He knew that the Englishman had once told a priest of his three greatest wishes: to serve and live with lepers, to die a martyr and to be buried in his Franciscan habit.

Full of grief, Gibbs made a point of returning to Bradburne's hut to recover his habit for safekeeping. But in all the drama that followed the murder, Gibbs forgot to dress the body in it. When he arrived at the funeral in Salisbury, he placed the habit on top of the coffin. It lay alongside three flowers which a friend of Bradburne had arranged there to symbolise his devotion to the Trinity: the Father, Son and Holy Ghost.

As the funeral progressed, the priest in charge noticed to his surprise that a drop of fresh blood had fallen from the coffin. He covered it with a cloth, but two more drops fell on the material. The scene was witnessed by both Father Gibbs and the local undertaker, who was horrified at his faulty workmanship. This was, after all, the funeral of a holy man.

After the ceremony, the coffin was opened for

inspection. There was no sign of any blood issuing from the body and the coffin walls were all clean and dry. Mouthing prayers, the undertaker and priests dressed Bradburne in his Franciscan habit, the last of his three wishes, and buried him.

Within weeks, local people were speaking of him as a saint. The story of the three wishes, three flowers and three drops of blood took on the status of a supernatural mystery and many bizarre stories began to emerge.

There was the woman who prayed to his memory and found herself cured of terminal cancer. And the man who claimed Bradburne had come to him in a dream to warn of the way his son would die. Others told how, after talking to him or praying for him, they were visited by swarms of bees or eagles, symbols of the Franciscan way of life.

John Bradburne prayer cards are now distributed across Zimbabwe. There is also a shrine to him at the leper colony which was his life's work. But it may be many years before the Vatican confirms him as a saint. Material for his beatification, submitted to the archbishop of Zimbabwe in 1986, was considered insufficient to make a final judgment.

VISIONS OF THE VIRGIN

One of the most vicious wars ever to have raged among those who were once fellow countrymen has left the former Yugoslavia deeply scarred. Cities and suburbs that once thrived with shops and shoppers, businesses and businessmen are now ghost towns. The countryside is pockmarked with bomb craters and the cemeteries are full as people who were once neighbours do their utmost to annihilate each other.

Yet in this hell on earth there is a little piece of heaven. For standing tall in the Croatian village of Medjugorje, in Bosnia-Herzegovina, is a peaceful twin-towered church unblemished by the conflict. It is a place of worship devoted to the sightings of the Blessed Virgin Mary which recur in and around the village.

Thousands of pilgrims flock there each year in the hope of witnessing for themselves one of the visions either at the church or at a nearby hilltop shrine. No matter that Medjugorje is just 20km (13 miles) from Mostar, where much violence has been centred. Roads from the town to the village are littered with wrecked cars and burnt-out trucks which tell the story of the war so far and its manifest dangers. The faithful have been prepared to travel from all over the world to the site without paying heed.

The first apparition of many happened on 25 June 1981. Six peasant children were startled at the sight of the Virgin Mary which appeared before them on a hillside outside the village. Speaking in Croatian, she told them she had 10 secrets to impart regarding the future of the world. The children returned to their homes, urging their parents and friends to pray and repent.

It was the day after the 10th anniversary of this first vision that war broke out in the region with the Croats fighting by Serbs and Muslims. Despite a profound faith, the Croatians on this occasion did not take the Blessed Virgin's call for peace to heart.

Yet Medjugorje itself has escaped much of the trauma of the war. The village is alive with the story of the captured Serb pilot who had been dispatched by his commanders to bomb the church. He told the Croats later that as he flew over his target, it was obscured with a luminous cloud. Filled with dread, the pilot decided he had to turn back. It was soon after that he was taken prisoner.

One villager who regularly sees the Blessed Virgin is Marijana Dragicevic. 'She is tall,' according to Dragicevic, 'a little taller than me, and very beautiful. She has rosy cheeks, blue eyes and long black hair – it goes in under a white veil but you see it come out again at the waist. On feast days she is dressed in gold but usually she wears a grey dress and a crown of stars.'

Now visitors talk of looking up into the sky and seeing a spinning sun. Out of the sun explodes a rainbow of colours and the face of the Virgin is clearly visible. Others have seen a bright red light hanging in the sky or enter a trance-like state as they receive her words.

Messages received by visionaries at Medjugorje are translated into different languages and flashed around the world. At church blessings, pilgrims keel over having been 'slain in the spirit'. They lie with their eyeballs flickering beneath heavy lids for anything up to half an hour. One British woman, Carmen Blackett, tells how her white rosary turned to gold when she visited Medjugorje. 'Then I brought my prayer group – 25 people – and all of theirs turned gold, too.'

It is stories like this, however, which have kept the Catholic authorities in Rome at arm's length. Pilgrimages to Medjugorje are still not officially sanctioned by the Vatican. But this has not stopped people from making them.

There has been an attempt by the Croatians to hijack the visions of the Virgin as a symbol of right-eousness in the conflict. One Franciscan friar in the region went as far as to say: 'You will have noticed that all our soldiers wear rosary beads round their necks. Rosary beads – that is why the Croatian soldier is not killing his enemy. He is forgiving.'

Yet there is another theory about why the Blessed Virgin chose to appear in Medjugorje. During the Second World War, Yugoslavia was occupied by the Nazis, with the Croats largely supporting the occupying forces. As a reward for their subservience, the Germans created a Croat state. Out of this new state came the ruling that all Serbs – ethnic enemies of the Croats – must either return to Serbia, convert to Catholicism or die.

This was no idle threat. On 6 August 1941 members of the Croatian militia, the Ustase, rounded up old men, women and children from the Serbian town of Prebilovici, just across the river from Medjugorje. After holding them prisoner for two days, the Ustase took the helpless civilians to a natural crater in the hills nearby and threw them in. Before dispatching them to their deaths, the Ustase broke their hands to stop them climbing to freedom.

In 1990 two Orthodox priests led some Serbian soldiers to the area to bless the site and exhume the bodies. It is said the remains of 300 Serb children and more than 200 women were brought out. Some claim the Blessed Virgin appears nearby in order that the Croatians should atone and heal the rifts in the communities.

A Canadian pilgrim, retired mechanic John Greensides, saw a vision of the Virgin Mary when he visited the shrine at Medjugorje. When he returned to his home in Marmora, Ontario, that too became a focus for pilgrimages. Photos taken at the farmhouse home purportedly reveal an image of the sun, with a face and a body emerging, surrounded by little angels.

The latest vision of the Virgin in Croatia is only the latest in two millennia of sightings. Perhaps the most famous of all occurred at Lourdes in France. In 1858 local girl Bernadette Soubirous, aged 14, saw the Blessed Virgin Mary 18 times at a grotto by the River Gave. At the 10th visitation, a spring began to flow there. The waters from it gained a reputation for healing the sick. At the age of 20, Bernadette became a nun. She died in 1879 and was canonised in 1933.

About 40,000 people now visit Lourdes every year. Although 6,000 claim to have been cured there, doctors are doubtful of at least some of the stories.

There are more recent instances of the Virgin's appearance. At Conyers, near Atlanta, Georgia, a young woman apparently saw her in the sky in 1988. Nancy Fowler reportedly had monthly conversations with the Virgin thereafter. Her claims of the vision appearing in the heavens have oft been repeated by others. Pilgrims have flocked there with cameras hoping to capture the vision on film.

Also in America, Theresa Lopez says she has

seen the Blessed Virgin on the second Sunday of every month since 1991 at Lookout Mountain in Colorado.

Stephen Marino is aiming to build a seven-storey housing complex plus an enormous chapel at Kettle River in Minnesota in accordance with the wishes of the Blessed Virgin. She imparted the instructions to him when she appeared before him near the town.

In the Philippines, 12-year-old Judiel Nieva claimed to have seen the Virgin Mary. In addition, a statue of her owned by his family apparently cried bloody tears. On 6 March 1993, Nieva claimed she would appear just after lunch. A crowd of more than 300,000 people gathered with him at its head and many concurred with Nieva that she had indeed manifested herself that afternoon.

WEREWOLVES

A 17-year-old boy had been attending seances in an attempt to invoke the spirit of his dead father. After each seance, the youth grew more and more morose. He confided to a friend that at one of the sessions the Devil himself had taken control of his soul. At another seance, believing that he was a black cat, he began pawing the table, nervously twitching all the while.

One of his closest classmates described his friend's 'possession' by evil forces: 'He told me his face and hands were changing colour and that he was changing into a werewolf. He would go quiet and then start growling. I told him to see his brother. He said he had a knife and was going to kill himself.'

Distraught beyond belief, the unfortunate youth took himself to the nearest crossroads to his home and stabbed himself through the heart. He chose the crossroads because in folklore death there is a sure way of preventing the wolf spirit rising again to prowl the earth.

A tale from the distant past? An example of superstition from mediaeval mid-Europe perhaps? Or a piece of B-movie fiction set in a mythical Transylvania?

No. The incident happened in the 1990s. The victim was an ordinary schoolboy, Andrew Prinfold. And the crossroads were near his home in Eccleshall, Staffordshire. Andrew stabbed himself through the heart in the absolute conviction that he was turning into a werewolf. His was a classic case of lycanthropy.

According to Chambers' *Encyclopedic English Dictionary*, lycanthropy means: 'In popular superstition, the power of changing from human shape into that of an animal, usually the most dangerous beast of the area. In Europe and northern Asia it is usually a wolf or bear, in India and other parts of Asia a tiger, and in Africa a leopard. Also a kind of madness in which the patient has fantasies of being a wolf.'

Part of the torment for such lycanthropes as Andrew Prinfold is that they tell themselves there is no earthly cure that will send them to rest – and so they set about finding unearthly ones. Other ways of escape from their werewolf persona include shooting themselves with a bullet made from inherited silver or being stabbed with a silver knife.

The study of lycanthropy is the only way in which medical science can today come to terms with the long-held beliefs in werewolf delusions and actual transformations. However, the activities of modern-day lycanthropes go only part of the way towards explaining the legend.

The werewolf has been a part of folklore for over
3,000 years.

Lycanthropy is from the Greek *lukos* for wolf and *anthropos* for man, and it was the philosophers of this civilisation who first made a serious study of the phenomenon – folklore accounts of were-wolfism predate the birth of Christ by 1,000 years.

Nowadays the term tends to be used to describe someone who is assumed to be mentally sick and believes he has assumed animal character-istics. The ancient Greeks, however, believed literal-ly that such a metamorphosis could take place. It was not until the 15th and 16th centuries, however, that the belief reached fever pitch in northern Europe.

By tradition, a werewolf will have sunken, staring eyes, perhaps eyebrows which join up on the bridge of the nose, hair growing on the palms of the hands and the 'Devil's Mark', a birthmark usually hidden from view. There may also be a long third finger, low-hung ears, fingernails shaped like almond nuts and a brownish tinge to all nails. In rural France it is still widely thought that a man sporting uncontrolled growth of a thumbnail is a wolf in human guise.

According to serious researches of the 15th and 16th centuries, a true werewolf is a person who can actually change his entire being into that of a wolf. Except for his larger size, human voice and eyes, he would appear little different from the actu-al animal. When captured, a werewolf often had his normal appearance explained away by the theory that these half-men, half-beasts could grow their fur on the inside of their skins!

Werewolf cultists believe that it is possible to be transformed into one by accident. This supposedly occurs through 'astral projection' – the phenomenon in which the soul is said to rise from the body and float freely across the earth at fantastic speed. Mystics claim they can do it at will. Many others have described the experience as something they remember after recovering from near death.

Whenever a soul is projected, the shell it leaves behind is in great danger of being taken over by a werewolf. This belief is probably linked to the old European custom of guarding a body from occupation by satanic spirits whenever a person has died between Christmas and Epiphany – a time when the forces of evil have much greater power on Earth.

Other supposed pathways to possession include sleeping outdoors in summer with the full moon shining straight on your face, or conceiving a child on the night of the full moon – in which case he or she is in danger of growing up a werewolf!

It all sounds so far-fetched that we tend to dismiss the werewolf delusion as mythology. Yet the difference between myth and legend is the degree of truth with which the story can be imbued – and it is obvious that reports of werewolfism are not just the chatter of country simpletons. The centuries-old sagas cannot be dismissed that easily.

In 1589 the most notorious werewolf of all time, Peter Stump, was arraigned in Cologne, Germany, accused of selling his soul to the Devil for the ability to transform himself into a wolf. For 25 years he roamed the countryside around Bedburg tearing innocent victims to shreds to satisfy his bloodlust. According to a contemporary account: 'He took such pleasure and delight in the shedding of blood that he would night and day walk the fields and perform extreme cruelties.'

His favoured victims were young girls, whom he captured and raped while in human form before 'changing into a wolf to tear them apart'. In just five years, he murdered 15 women and children, including two girls who were pregnant. In some cases, he tore out their hearts and ate them 'panting hot and raw'.

Stump was aided and abetted in his savagery by his mistress, Katherine Trompin, and by his daughter, Beell, with whom he was committing incest. Beell bore him a son but such was his stomach-churning depravity that he ate the infant – and declared the brains as 'a most savoury and dainty delicious' meal.

Until his capture, limbs of his victims were found almost weekly in the fields around Bedburg, whose villagers dared not leave their homes unless armed or protected. Stump's atrocities upon the innocent finally ended when, ironically, a pack of hunting dogs led their masters to him in their search for what they believed to be a real wolf. When hunted down, he is said to have still been in the guise of a werewolf.

In court, he was predictably found guilty and the judge ordered: 'His body shall be laid on a wheel and with red hot burning pincers in several places to have the flesh pulled off him from the bones; after that his legs and arms to be broken with a wooden hatchet, afterwards to have his head struck from his body; then to have his carcass burned to ashes.'

After watching the burning of Stump's headless corpse, his mistress and daughter were also burned at the stake.

It was France, not Germany, which was the hot-bed of werewolf activity, however. In a hundred years between the 15th and 16th centuries, no fewer than 30,000 cases were reported to the authorities. Some of these could be attributed to rabies, prevalent at the time, and which turns its victims into aggressive madmen.

One of the worst cases was the nameless Werewolf of Châlons, arraigned in Paris in 1598 on murder charges so sickening that all documents were destroyed after the case. Referred to in records only as the 'Demon Tailor', even his real name has become lost in history.

In the 15th and 16th centuries belief in werewolves reached fever pitch in northern Europe.

In human guise, the demonic tailor lured customers into his shop, where he would subject them to gory perversions before cutting their throats and preparing the flesh to eat. The monster's despicable habits also took him to woods around the city where he would 'assume the form of a wolf' and prey on innocent walkers. The total number of his victims was never properly established but there is little doubt that it ran into dozens. When his house was raided, barrels of human bones immersed in bleach, along with fragments of limbs, were found in the cellar. He went to the stake cursing and blaspheming to the last.

When he was sent to the stake the day after his trial, a huge crowd gathered to watch his final moments. And unlike many another convicted werewolf who repented of his sins as the first flames licked around his legs, the Demon Tailor betrayed no hint of remorse. He could be heard cursing and blaspheming to the very end.

In 16th-century France, one judge was feared almost as much as werewolves themselves. He was Henri Boguet, supreme judge of the St Claude district in Burgundy and author of the French witch-hunters' 'bible' *Discours des Sorciers*.

His favourite method of obtaining confessions was to strap accused werewolves and witches to the wheel three or four at a time. When lowered close to the ground and turned, flesh would be ripped off and bones crushed. The victims, still agonisingly alive, would usually confess to anything – even if it meant certain death at the stake. Other means of questioning included the rack, branding, whipping, crucifixion, or tearing at the flesh with white-hot pincers.

Among those who suffered Boguet's tortures was a rare, female 'werewolf'. Clauda Gaillard, who had supposedly been seen turning herself into a beast, received Boguet's judgment: 'Common report was against her. No one ever saw her shed a single tear, whatever effort might be made to cause her to shed tears.' She was burned at the stake.

Boguet believed werewolves could shed no more than three tears from their right eye. If an accused person wept profusely under torture, they had a chance of being freed. Perversely, many victims found that, in their pain and terror, no tears would come.

There can have been few more appalling sights in the annals of human misery than Henry Boguet and his measuring phials containing the tears of the tortured. He would inspect them at his leisure. One perhaps barely damp with moisture would be taken as unequivocal proof of sorcery. Another might be full of tears – but perhaps shed from the wrong eye.

In his *Discours*, Boguet urged other judges to put his tear theory to the test in sorcery and werewolf trials. He wrote:

'The doctors esteem it one of the strongest presumptions that exist as a test of the crime of sorcery. I wish to report what has come to my knowledge. All the sorcerers whom I have examined in quality of judge have never shed tears in my presence; or, indeed, if they have shed them it has been so parsimoniously that no notice was taken of them.

'I say this with regard to those who seemed to weep, but I doubt if their tears were not feigned. I am at least well assured that those tears were wrung from them with the greatest efforts. This was shown by the efforts which the accused made to weep, and by the small number of tears which they shed. Yet if I spoke to them in private they shed tears and wept with all possible vehemence.

'The same happened when they confessed. They then showed themselves more lively and joyous than they had previously been, as if they had been delivered from a great burden. Besides it is probable that sorcerers do not shed tears, since tears serve principally to penitents to wash away and cleanse their sins.

'Nevertheless, if you demand of sorcerers why they do not shed tears, they answer you that it is impossible for them to weep because they have the heart too much oppressed at seeing themselves disgraced by the imputation of a crime so detestable as that of sorcery.'

Not all werewolf cases are from darker ages.

At the end of the last century, a professor from Oxford University was staying with his wife and a friend in a lakeside cottage in Merionethshire, Wales, where he chanced upon a massive skull, apparently from a large hound. That night, as the men took a walk, the wife heard scratching noises from outside the cottage and saw through the window a hideous part-man-part-beast scrabbling to get inside. She fainted. Upon their return, her husband and friend revived the woman and lay in wait for the beast's return. According to Montague Summers, author of *The Werewolf*:

'That night, having made all secure and extinguished the lamps, the two men sat up quietly armed with stout sticks and a gun. The hours passed slowly until, when all was darkest and most lonely, the soft thud of cushioned paws was heard on the gravel outside and nails scratched at the kitchen window. To their horror, in a stale phosphorescent light they saw the hideous mask of a wolf, with the eyes of a man, glaring through the glass, eyes that were red with hellish rage.

'Snatching the gun, they rushed to the front door but it had seen their movement and was away in a moment. As they issued from the house, a shadowy undefined shape slipped through the open gate and in the stars they could just see a huge animal making towards the lake, into which it disappeared, nor did a ruffle cross the surface of the water.

'Early the next morning the professor took the skull and rowing a little way out from shore flung it as far as he could into the deepest part of the water. The werewolf never returned to his hauntings again.'

Summers concluded that the manifestation was a werewolf spirit, condemned to haunt the ground where his bones lay.

A more recent werewolf scare occurred in 1957 at a newly-built nurses' hostel in Singapore. The young nurses were so frightened by man-beast sightings that they barricaded their dormitory. But one girl still reported: 'I woke to find a horrible face, with hair reaching down to the bridge of the nose, glaring down at me. The creature had two long, protruding red fangs. I saw him clearly because the room was bathed in moonlight. I tried to scream but could not. I staggered into the corner and collapsed.'

Police put the incidents down to student pranks – until the girl revealed neat puncture marks on her wrists. They then blamed the visitation on an occult brotherhood which had performed a wolfic ceremony on one of its members. Ancient sorcery had reared its head again in the 20th century...

PAST LIVES

The knowledge of having lived a past life, in another age, in another culture or even as a member of the opposite sex, is a gift which many have claimed. There is no rhyme or reason, nor any scientific evidence, to prove or disprove people's beliefs that they were once soldiers in Caesar's army, ladies in waiting to Elizabeth I of England or attendants of long-dead Egyptian pharaohs. Such experiences are not the exclusive domain of cranks or eccentrics. Many people, noted for their rationality in everyday life, have been subject to this strangest of experiences.

The most famous – and certainly the best chronicled – account of past lives concerns the amazing Joan Grant. This wealthy daughter of a privileged English upper-class family detailed astounding experiences as a priestess-pharaoh in ancient Egypt, another Egyptian noble, this time a man, an Italian singer of the 16th century and an English girl of the 19th century.

What singled Joan Grant out from the ranks of many who claim to have lived past lives was the mysterious power which she seemed to possess. She categorised her experiences into two types: 'far memory' dreams, which transcended space and time, and 'true' dreams, the premonitions of which came true.

Joan Grant was born in 1907 and raised in a gracious manner in those last heady days before the conflagration of the Great War burst upon the world. She spent the war years in England and it was when she was nine years old that she first displayed her uncanny powers.

She came down to breakfast one morning, troubled, as she had been for many months, by frightening war dreams in which she smelt the stench an heard the fearful noise of battle. On this particular morning there was a soldier in uniform with her father, and she said to him:

'Somehow I know you will not laugh at me. Last night I was with a man called McAndrew when he was killed. I can describe the regimental badge although I cannot remember the name of the regiment, except that it was not an English one. And I can tell you the nickname of his trench.'

The soldier returned to the front with this eerie prophecy indelibly stamped on his mind. Some weeks later he wrote back to the girl's father:

'For heaven's sake don't laugh at the child. I cannot attempt an explanation, but I have checked what she said. A battalion of that regiment (part of the Canadian Machine Gun Corps) went over the top on a night attack a few hours before she told me about it. A private called McAndrew was among

Joan Grant.

those killed. She was even correct about the name of the front line trench.'

From then onwards, Joan Grant's other lives manifested themselves in many different forms. One of the visitors at the family home in Hampshire was the distinguished Cambridge professor C G Lamb, who had been great friend of the little girl's grandmother, Jennie Marshall. There was an extraordinary bond between the two, and Joan told him one day that Jennie, who had been a concert pianist of some talent, was giving her lessons – even though she was long dead.

The professor did not scoff at her, but listened intently as the girl sat at her piano and played. Professor Lamb looked quite perplexed after she had finished playing and said:

'Extraordinary, quite extraordinary, but completely evidential. What you have just played was often played to me by your grandmother. I have not heard it since she died. Only one copy of that music ever existed, given to the tsar of Russia who sent it on to your grandmother. I happen to know that that music manuscript was burned two years before you were born.'

When she was 16, Joan met the great science fiction novelist H G Wells, who was captivated by her powers. He advised her to keep her own counsel about her 'dream lives' until she felt able to deal with the ridicule and scorn which would inevitably be directed at her by non-believers.

Joan married – but her husband died in a shooting accident, which she had uncannily foretold in a chilling dream, similar to her First World War experience. It was her second husband who undertook the task of helping her write down her experiences.

In one of these, she was a French sailor aboard a Channel vessel which burst into flames. She said the name of the ship was the *Atlantic* and that it was heading for Cherbourg. Late that same day a ship called the *Atlantique* caught fire in the channel en route to Cherbourg and many people died.

Joan's most startling past-life experience was as Sekeeta, a priestess-pharaoh. She wrote a book about it in 1937 called *Winged Pharaoh*, in which she described in astonishing detail the lives lived by the ancient Egyptians 4,000 years before. The book was hailed as a magnificent historical novel – except that Joan Grant did not research one single fact. It all came from her far-memory dreams that she had lived there all that time ago.

Later she published two more books, *Eyes of Horus* and *Lord of the Horizon,* which chronicled her experiences as Ra-ab Hotep, an Egyptian servant of the pharaoh who lived 1,000 years after Sekeeta.

She also 'died' as a witch in the late middle ages in Germany and had her wrists cut in Roman times by the man who was later to become her third husband in modern times, Dr Denys Kelsey.

Joan Grant believed that her past lives were more than merely fascinating experiences and could be of real use. She believed that the problems and afflictions of this physical, earthly life could be understood and conquered by drawing on the experience of past lives.

Knowledge of past lives is no new phenomenon. Many religions hold true to the belief of reincarnation – often in the form of other animal species. The difference nowadays is that a new tool is often employed to take a subject back to a previous existence: hypnosis.

The most famous case of regression by hypnosis was that of Bridey Murphy – the alter ego of a 29-year-old Wisconsin housewife. In 1952 an amateur hypnotist named Morey Bernstein regressed the housewife, Virginia Tighe, back to her previous existence as Bridey in 18th century Cork, Ireland. In a lilting Irish brogue, 'Bridey' told how she was born Bridget Murphy in 1798, the daughter of a middle-class Protestant family, and in 1818 married a Catholic, Brian McCarthy.

In her role as Bridey, Mrs Tighe could describe her schoolroom, her wedding, the wedding guests and the stagecoach journey she took on her honeymoon to Belfast, where she and her husband started a new life. Virginia Tighe had never set foot on

Irish soil and had no Irish relatives, yet her descriptions were entirely accurate. For instance, the place names on the route from Cork to Belfast were on no modern map – yet historical research revealed that they had all existed.

She also used colloquialisms that had long been forgotten. Bridey went 'ditching' in Belfast shops named Carrigan's and Farr's. 'Ditching' is old Irish for purchasing, and the two now-defunct stores were proved to have been open for business in the early 1800s.

More eerily, Bridey Murphy talked in matter-of-fact tones about her own funeral. In the last of a year-long series of regressions, she told how she died aged 66 after falling and breaking her hip. Bridey was particularly taken by the mournful sound of the 'uillean pipes' traditionally played at Irish funerals of that time. Coming out of hypnosis and returning to her latter-day life as a Wisconsin housewife, Mrs Virginia Tighe had not the faintest notion what 'uillean pipes' were!

The story of Bridey Murphy became known around the world because of a movie made about the strange, hypnotic experiment. Other less sensationally presented stories can be just as intriguing.

One of the most credible past-life experiences was that related by retired British Army captain Arthur Flowerdew, who had led an uneventful life and never travelled farther than Europe. Yet he was

Diana, Princess of Wales, is another who
believes that she has lived before.

convinced he had lived before as a soldier in the Jordanian city of Petra 2,200 years ago

He explained to an author writing a book about his experiences that as a boy at the seaside he picked up red and amber stones, thinking they looked familiar. He said they looked like the stones of a city hewn out of rock, and along with them came mental images of a city cut out of the cliffs, of men in flowing Biblical robes, and the terrible pain he endured from a huge Syrian spear being plunged into his body.

The author, Joan Forman, checked his account and found it tallied with historical descriptions of the city of Petra. Flowerdew was later shown colour slides of the ruins taken on a holiday in 1964, and stunned Joan Forman with uncanny descriptions of what was next to the images – things that were not visible on the actual slides themselves.

It will always remain a mystery as to how well-to-do suburban people like Joan Grant, a Wisconsin housewife and a gentle, retired English army officer could relive the exciting, violent lives of people who lived on earth hundreds and sometimes thousands of years ago. Yet there is no shortage of adherents to the belief in reincarnation.

Even Diana, Princess of Wales, believes that she has lived a past life. In the notorious 'Squidgy' phone call, when she was recorded sighing words of love to a male friend, Princess Di referred to meeting a Bishop. This is how it went:

Diana: 'I know this sounds crazy, but I've lived before.'

Bishop: 'How do you know?'

Diana: 'Because I'm a wise old thing.'

Stars of the world of entertainment seem more prone than most to experiences and senses of a life beyond the grave. Is the fact that so many believe they are living out a 'second life' merely an indication that actors, actresses and other showbusiness stars have more overactive imaginations than mere mortals? Or is it proof of reincarnation?

Hollywood, for instance, is nicknamed the 'Dream Factory' – and its stars regularly go before the cameras to act out dramas of days gone by. But many have lived out other images of a past age. These are not products of the Dream Factory, nor dreams at all – but seemingly incontrovertible evidence of past-life experiences.

Movie star Glenn Ford was one among many who experienced overwhelming feelings of having lived previous lives. Ford, a God-fearing man, had his beliefs turned upside down by experiencing not just one past life, but two.

In 1978 Ford agreed to undergo hypnosis at his home in Beverley Hills. While he was in a hypnotic trance, he recalled working as a Colorado cowboy in the days of the Wild West. He said his name was Charlie Bill and that he worked for a rancher called Charlie Goodnight.

He spoke of long hard days in the saddle, gave detailed descriptions of the food that cowhands of the day ate, and spoke of how he was eventually shot and killed by rustlers. The session was tape-recorded for academics at the University of California to study.

They went to Colorado – and unearthed evidence that two men with the names he related had lived in the last century, but could discover little else about them. A second session some months later proved to be much more informative.

The second experiment was conducted at the university itself where Ford, then 61, once again responded well to hypnosis

This time he was not riding the range as Charlie Bill – but emerged as a Scottish piano teacher named Charles Stuart. 'I teach piano to young flibbertigibets,' said Ford, using a quaint old English word for rascals, not commonly heard in 20th century southern California. He also played a few notes on the piano while under hypnosis – although when he heard the tapes later he confessed that he had never been taught to play the instrument.

The Californian researchers this time made the journey to Elgin in Scotland, where they discovered the grave of Charles Stuart, who died in 1840. On their return they showed Ford a photograph of his

Four past lives for Rambo - including that of a 1930s boxer.

Martin Sheen believes that he has lived before - as a US cavalry officer.

past-life burial place, and he said: 'That shook me up really bad. I felt immediately that it was the place I was buried.'

Other stars have had strange past-life experiences which have had a permanent effect on them. Tough actor Martin Sheen believes that his fear of horses is due to his once having been a cruel US cavalry officer. He suffered a panic attack when his children suggested that they take up riding.

Sheen's costar in *The Believers*, Helen Shaver, believes that she was once a Greek princess who in 579 BC made love to her adopted son – who then strangled her.

Sylvester Stallone believes that he lived not one but four separate lives. In two of them he met a violent end – as a nobleman guillotined in the French Revolution and as a boxer killed by a punch in the 1930s.

Catherine Oxenberg believes that stomach pains she once suffered were the result of experiments carried out on her in a past life as a victim of Nazi concentration camp doctors.

Singers have also had their share of multiple lives. Country legend Loretta Lynn relives a nightmare existence in which she supports a dying husband and three hungry children while living in conditions of appalling poverty. She says:

'I see myself running home up an old gravel road, barefoot and wearing a dirty cotton dress. My

Willie Nelson, a professional gunfighter in an earlier
life?

house is a shack; I don't know how anybody could live in a place like that. My kids are triplets who have just started walking. They scream while my husband lies in bed moaning.'

Loretta has also spoken of another past life, in no happier circumstances. She describes being in 'a kind of trance' more than once, when she saw a hillside filled with horses and Indians. She continues:

'All the Indians have their warpaint on. I know the Indian on the horse up front is my husband, and that he is the chief because he has a long feathered headdress all the way down his back. I am standing beside my husband in a buckskin skirt and pigtailed hair as he and his braves prepare to go out into the valley.

'I am saying goodbye to my husband when all of a sudden a shot rings out. He slumps forward and falls off the horse. I scream and start running towards the tepees.'

Fellow Country star Willie Nelson (who, unlike Loretta, does indeed wear a pigtail) also has visions from the Wild West. He has talked of being 'fried' in the electric chair after a career as a professional gunfighter.

Canadian singer Helen Reddy, who is a fervent believer in psychic phenomena, is another who claims to have lived hundreds of past lives – and even to have seen her own death. The 46-year-old star said:

Catherine Oxenburg believes that she suffered at the hands of the Nazis in an earlier life.

'I'm in a hospital bed and my father, who has long been dead of alcoholism, comes to me wearing a white doctor's coat, and it's like he's sneaked into the hospital to see me. He says: "I've come to take you home, your mom's waiting for you." I feel no fear of death. I just get up out of the bed and go with him. I'm very happy because I feel like I'm going home to see everybody. I remember it all so clearly because I was so peaceful and happy.'

During meditation and hypnosis sessions, Helen has claimed to have been a page at a joust in 13th century England, a duchess, a maid, a gypsy palm reader in Egypt and a potter in the Middle East.

In yet another experience, she claimed to have been a trader crossing a Persian desert when he – for that experience was, like many of her's, as a man – was ambushed. She recounted:

'I feel tremendous fear and can hear horses' hooves coming. The next thing I see is someone coming into my tent on horseback. He has one of those curved knives and he slices off my head.'

When she was 12, Helen claimed to have had an 'out of body' experience, when her consciousness left her body. She said she was in a school assembly when she suddenly saw brown spots in front of eyes. She looked down and saw a body on the floor, someone who had apparently fainted. It took her several disbelieving moments before she realised that it was her own body she was staring at. 'It scared the hell out of me,' she confessed.

FACES FROM BEYOND

The pen of Coral Polge darts across her sketch pad. In lightning time, a face appears. Then distinctive features were added. In minutes the portrait is completed. It will never be handed over to the 'model' whose likeness she has has perfected, however, for Coral is a psychic artist who claims to tune in to the world beyond the grave. The uncannily accurate pictures she draws so casually on her pad are of the dead. She does not recognise them herself, because she has never seen them before.

It is the amazed friends and relatives of the dead who would identify the portraits at the sittings and public demonstrations Coral gave all over the world. In her lifetime of practising her uncanny art, Coral estimated that she has sketched a staggering 100,000 portraits from beyond the grave.

'I never know who I am drawing', she said. 'It could be anyone who is dead and who wants in particular to communicate with someone who is with me.

'I never see the people as I draw them. I feel as if I become them. Once, at a demonstration in London, I seemed to be riding a bicycle as I drew a portrait of a young woman. I could literally feel myself on a bike with a basket full of shopping on the front. But I had great trouble with her likeness, because I kept wondering what had happened to my face. I had to alter the drawing two or three times. A woman in the audience recognised it as her daughter who had died in a cycling accident. She had gone over the handlebars and landed on her face.'

On another occasion, Coral was on stage drawing a girl's face when she suddenly stopped, clutching her throat and made a choking sound. 'I could feel terrible contractions in my throat,' she said. 'I felt as if I'd been poisoned. Then a woman in the audience recognised the sketch. She said it was her daughter who had been poisoned by carbon monoxide fumes.'

'Sometimes when I draw suicides or people who have died violently I go through agony.'

Coral had never even heard of spiritualism when in 1946, at the age of 20, a friend suggested a healer might be able to help her mother's arthritis. 'The healer didn't cure her,' she said, 'but she did her more good than doctors had. That led me to my first meeting at a spiritualist church, where a medium gave me a message from a great uncle I'd been very fond of that I would be a psychic artist.

'Quite honestly, I thought it was a load of rubbish. I was a very average commercial artist at the time, but some friends persuaded me to try to find out something about psychic art, which wasn't easy because it's a very rare thing. I spent some years experimenting, and gradually I got the feeling that someone in the psychic world was guiding me. Then I found people beginning to recognise my drawings as individuals they had known.'

'I have two or three spirit guides. The main one is an 18th century French pastel artist, Maurice Quentin de la Tour. I discovered this when one day I drew a figure in a powdered wig and lace ruffs whom I felt sure was connected with my psychic art. An art expert friend identified it as an exact likeness of Maurice.'

British-based, Coral travelled the world for more than 30 years, often working with a clairvoyant whom, as she sketches, passes on verbal messages from the 'sitter' to someone in her audience. She first hit the headlines in 1977 when, at a public demonstration, she drew a picture of a smiling, neat looking young man.

'I had no idea who it was,' said Carol. But suddenly a woman jumped from the audience and cried out in recognition of a friend.

Nanette Morgan had identified a young soldier who had been killed in Northern Ireland three months earlier. While on leave in his hometown of Sittingborne, Kent, Second-Lieutenant Michael Simpson, aged 21, had told Nanette that he had a premonition he would be killed when he returned to duty. He told her: 'I know this will be the end when I go back. But if you consult a medium, I will return and give you cast-iron evidence.'

Shortly after arriving back in Northern Ireland, Michael Simpson was shot dead. Nanette went to a clairvoyant who told her Michael was in the spirit world. Later the same day she went to one of Coral's demonstrations and watched in amazement as Michael's face appeared on her sketch pad.

Nanette said: 'Michael and I had made a pact, but I could scarcely believe it when Coral drew an exact likeness of him. I don't think I have ever cried so much. It was wonderful, heart-stopping evidence that he had kept his pact with me. Michael must have been very happy that he was able to get through to me and prove his love in such an incredible way.'

One of Coral's most memorable cases involved another young man who had had a fatal premonition. Roger West, of Bradford, West Yorkshire, had a premonition that he would die before he was 25 – in fact, he died the day before his 25th birthday. Later, his mother had a sitting with Coral, who produced a drawing of him. Soon afterwards the woman visited a woman medium Coral had never met. Through her, the son said: 'I hope you liked the picture.'

Housewife Rosemary Raithky had a private sitting with Coral, hoping for a drawing of her dead mother. 'Her mother didn't come through,' Coral said. 'I got her father instead. He looks a forceful character, and he probably insisted on being the one to make contact.'

At a private sitting for opera singer Grace Brooks, Coral found herself drawing another singer, Maria Malibran who died in 1836. All Coral could tell Grace was: 'This is a Spanish singer named Maria.' At the British Museum, Grace found a portrait of Maria Malibran that bore a striking resemblance to Coral's drawing.

Coral once visited Brooklands, the famous prewar motor racing circuit southwest of London, where, although cracked and overgrown, many locals still hear the roar of engines and the squeal of tyres. Suddenly she sketched a hawk-faced man and told her tour guide: 'This man raced here, although not motorcars. He was not killed but died from natural causes.'

Her companion replied: 'You have drawn a man called O'Donovan. He raced motorcycles and died a few months ago from natural causes.'

Coral said: 'I can't draw people to order. If someone asks for a particular person, I'll ask my guides if they can get them, but it doesn't often work. Some times I go through patches where I can't draw at all and I begin to think I've lost the gift. Other times the results are so brilliantly accurate it's almost frightening.'

'People have told me I could make a fortune if I chose. But I'm not doing it for the money. There are greater rewards. Every now and then someone gets a picture of their mother or their son, and then they know their loved one has landed safely in the next world. That gives me more satisfaction than money ever could.'

Coral Polge always realised the power – and the dangers – of her amazing link with the world beyond the grave. She said: 'One word of warning. People feel tempted to try things like psychic art as a game. But like ouija boards and planchette, it can be dangerous. You need a good, trained medium to guide you. Otherwise it's like answering your door on a dark night and saying "Come in" before you know who it is.'

PREMONITIONS AND PROPHECIES

The *Titanic* was the grandest ship of her age, a veritable floating palace that combined grace, elegance and size with the latest in engineering and design. She was built for the great transatlantic runs and her owners and captain boasted that she was unsinkable.

Fourteen years before her maiden voyage to New York, Morgan Robertson wrote a book called *Futility* in which he told the story of a luxurious liner, the *Titan*. He described how the vessel put to sea with insufficient lifeboats, how it was gashed beneath the waterline by a gigantic iceberg, and how it sank with terrible loss of life.

On 10 April 1912, on her maiden voyage, the doomed *Titanic* slid beneath the waves, her fate paralleling that of the fictional *Titan*, in what must be one of the most uncanny cases of unconscious premonition ever known.

Prophecies or premonitions of what the future has in store have been with us since the dawn of time. And they have come true with disturbing regularity. History's most famous prophecy came from the ancient seer Vestritius Spurinna, who whispered

**Julius Caesar: proof that forewarned is not necess-
arily forearmed.**

the immortal words 'Beware the Ides of March' to Caesar in 44 BC. That was indeed the day on which the conspirators of ancient Rome killed their emperor as he walked in the Forum.

Britain's most famous foreteller of the future was Mother Shipton, wife of a carpenter in Yorkshire. She lived from 1488 until 1561 and during that time foretold Cardinal Wolsey's arrest for treason, the reign of Queen Elizabeth I and the beheading of Mary Queen of Scots. In a poem which many believe to foretell the arrival of cars, submarines, radios and metal ships, she wrote:

Around the world, thoughts shall fly,
In the twinkling of an eye,
Under water men shall walk,
Shall ride, and sleep and even talk,
Carriages without horses shall go,
And accidents fill the world with woe,
In water, iron shall float,
As easily as a wooden boat.

History, however, credits the French physician Nostradamus as the greatest seer of all. If his last prediction proves to be accurate, the world will be plunged into its bloodiest ever war in 1999, from which few will emerge alive.

Nostradamus was born Michel de Notredame in a town in southwest France. A Jew by birth, he was brought up under the auspices of the Catholic church and its teachings. He changed his name

Mother Shipton, Britain's most famous foreteller.

when he was a medical student early in the 16th century, and became renowned for his work as a physician. But his real love lay in the paranormal, in clairvoyancy and astrology. When his wife and two children died, victims of the Great Plague, he became a traveller. He wandered around Europe making predictions which seemed to come true with astonishing accuracy.

While in Italy, he fell to his knees at the feet of a young priest who was walking along a pathway towards him. The priest thought he was mad, but Nostradamus proclaimed that one day he would be a great man in the Catholic church. That same priest, Felici Peretti, was ordained as Pope Sixtus V 50 years later.

In 1547 Nostradamus settled in Provence, remarried, and started to write down his major prophecies. He wrote in curious rhyming riddles which, though heavy with symbolism, were often open to interpretation. This, Nostradamus said, had a twofold purpose. One, he would not be accused of witchcraft and two, his readers would be entertained and not be too frightened by the true weight of what he was saying would happen in the future. These are some of his amazing predictions.

The young lion shall overcome the old,
In a warlike field in a single fight,
In a golden cage, he will pierce the eye,
Two wounds in one, then suffer a cruel death.

This is Nostradamus's prediction of the death of Henry II of France in 1559, wounded in the throat and eye during a joust – 'Two wounds in one' – who died in agony 10 days afterwards.

'The great plague of the maritime city shall not cease until death is avenged for the blood of the just, taken and condemned, though innocent, and the Great Dame, outraged by feigning saints.'

Historians have deciphered this as a prophecy of the plague that ravaged London in 1665. St Paul's was the cathedral, given its old French name of Dame. The 'just' is said to be a reference to King Charles I beheaded in 1649. And the 'feigning saints' are the Puritans of the age.

One of his most accurate predictions foretells the fate of London in the Great Fire of 1666. (Again, the Old Dame refers to St Paul's.):

The blood of the just shall be required
of London,
Burned by fire in thrice twenty and six,
The Old Dame shall fall from her high place,
And many edifices of the same sect shall
be destroyed.

He predicted the arrival of Napoleon in France from Corsica, prophesied the outbreak of the Spanish Civil War – accurately giving the names of the opposing sides' leaders – and predicted the emergence of Adolf Hitler, although he called him 'Hister'.

A leader of Great Germanies,
Who will come to give help which is only
counterfeit,
He will stretch the borders of Germany,
And will cause France to be divided into
two parts.
Living fire and death hidden in globes will
be loosed, horrible and terrible,
By night, the enemy will reduce cities to dust.

These references to globes clearly predict the advent of bombs and bombing raids by night on cities such as London and Berlin.

His most disturbing prophecy has yet to come to pass – his prediction of a great war in 1999. He forecast that a 'yellow race' would invade Europe and of 'blood and corpses' covering the land. He said the war to end all wars would culminate in 'the year 1999 and seven months, when from the sky will come the great king of terror'

One must hope that on this occasion Nostradamus will be proved wrong. But it is a prediction mirrored by the strange American clairvoyant Jeane Dixon, who foretold a great war beginning in the late 1980s and ending in 1999.

Jeane Dixon became a celebrity in America for her seemingly remarkable ability to predict certain things about President John F Kennedy. In 1952 she claimed that she had a vision of a 'blue-eyed Democrat entering the White House.' She said he would be there in 1960 – and that his life would end in assassination. Her prophecies, as we now know came true on both counts.

Carole Lombard, the actress, was fascinated by Jeane Dixon and had an audience with her. She warned the movie star not to take a flight within the following six weeks because it was dangerous. Lombard insisted that she had to take a plane because of pressure of work. It was to cost her her life. Three days after her audience with Jeane Dixon, she was killed in a plane crash.

Jeane Dixon also predicted President Kennedy's assassination in Dallas, on the very day it happened. She awoke on 22 November saying: 'This is the day it will happen.' It did.

But on that morning it seems that the president himself had an uncanny premonition of what was going to happen to him. He told his wife: 'If someone wants to shoot me from a window, with a rifle, I can't stop him. So let's not worry about him.' That was exactly the way he was to die.

Five years later, in an uncanny double-take of that premonition, his widow predicted of her brother-in-law Robert Kennedy: 'I know he is going to die the same way as my husband.' He, too, was shot dead.

Not all premonitions are made by clairvoyants like Nostradamus or by well-known people. In 1966 a Welsh schoolgirl named Eryl Jones told her

The dreadful events at Aberfan shocked the nation.

mother that she had walked to school in Aberfan, but that the school was no longer there. 'Something black had come over it,' she told her mother. Two days later, a moving black mountain of coal slag slid on to the school, killing 144 pupils and teachers.

COINCIDENCES

What makes a 'coincidence' occur? Consider the amazing links between the assassinations of US Presidents John F Kennedy and Abraham Lincoln.

An exact century separated the two presidents' elections to Congress. They were also elected President exactly 100 years apart. Lincoln's secretary was called John and Kennedy's secretary was called Lincoln. Kennedy's killer, Lee Harvey Oswald, was born exactly 100 years after Lincoln's killer, John Wilkes Booth.

Both presidents were killed by bullets fired by Southerners. Both were shot through the back of the head. Both had their wives beside them. Both assassinations were on a Friday. Neither assassin lived to stand trial. Lincoln died in Ford's Theatre; Kennedy died in a Ford-built Lincoln Continental. Both Presidents were succeeded by Southerners named Johnson, who were also born exactly 100 years apart.

On 8 April 1865, three days before the murder of Lincoln, one of his aides, Colonel Ward Lamon, jotted down a dream related to him by the president himself:

'I went from room to room; no living person

There are amazing links between Abraham Lincoln's
death and that of John F Kennedy.

Both Kennedy and Lincoln were assassinated on a Friday and succeeded by Southerners named Johnson.

Seconds after the bullets and President
Kennedy has been assassinated.

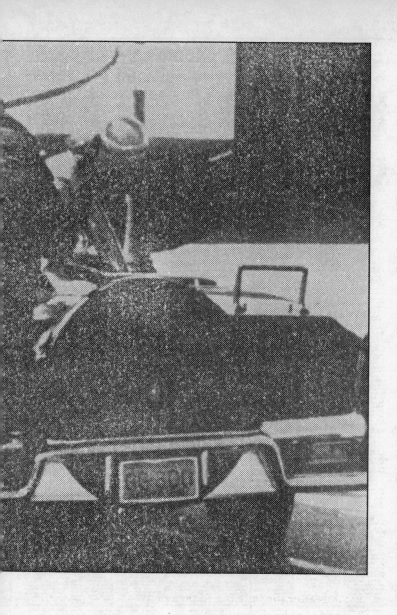

Johnson Takes
Nation's Helm.
Pages 4 and 5

The Dallas Morning News

John F. Kennedy
Life History,
Pages 16 and 17

VOL. 115—NO. 54   DALLAS, TEXAS, SATURDAY, NOVEMBER 23, 1963 — 38 PAGES IN 4 SECTIONS   PRICE 5 CENTS

KENNEDY SLAIN ON DALLAS STREET

* * *   * * *   * * *   * * *   * * *

JOHNSON BECOMES PRESIDENT

Receives Oath on Aircraft

Lyndon B. Johnson

Gov. Connally Resting Well

Impact Shattering To World Capitals

Pro-Communist Charged With Act

Four Hours in Surgery

Friendly Crowd Cheered Kennedy

FUNERAL FOR PRESIDENT WILL BE HELD ON MONDAY

John F. Kennedy

GRAY CLOUDS WENT AWAY

Day Began as Auspiciously As Any in Kennedy's Career

was in sight, but the same mournful sounds of distress met me as I passed along... I kept on until I walked to the East Room, which I entered. There I met with a sickening surprise. Before me was a catafalque, on which rested a corpse wrapped in funeral vestments ... "Who is dead in the White House?" I demanded of one of the soldiers. "The president," was his answer. "He was killed by an assassin!"'

Lincoln told one of his guards on the day he was murdered: 'I believe there are men who want to take my life and I have no doubt that they will do it. If it is to be done, it is impossible to prevent it.'

Likewise, Kennedy told his wife Jackie and aide Ken O'Donnell on the day of his assassination, 22 November 1963: 'If somebody wants to shoot me from a window with a rifle, nobody can stop it. So why worry about it?'

The parallels between the two assassinations prove not only the paranormal nature of coincidence but also that there is a fine line between coincidence and premonition (as studied in the previous chapter). Is it premonition, prophecy, precognition, extrasensory perception or some other psychic sense 'from the other side' that creates coincidences?

Take, for instance, the case of the lead coffin of an actor who died on tour at Galveston, Texas, and which was swept to sea in a hurricane. The coffin floated 2,000 miles to Prince Edward Island – the Canadian actor's home where it was intended to be transported.

Another instance was Edgar Allan Poe's tale of shipwrecked sailors who kill and eat a cabin boy named Richard Parker. Fifty years later shipwrecked sailors killed and ate a cabin boy named Richard Parker.

Even more intriguing is the story of Henry Ziegland who in 1893 jilted his fiancee. The girl then committed suicide. The girl's brother, vowing to avenge his sister's death, came after Ziegland with a pistol and shot him. The brother then committed suicide. Ziegland, however, had not been killed. He had only been dazed by the bullet, which grazed his face before embedding itself in a tree.

Twenty years later, Ziegland decided to cut down the tree, which adjoined his home in Honey Grove, Texas. So large had it grown that he decided to blast it out of the ground with dynamite. The explosion sent the old bullet flying through the air – and straight through Ziegland's head, killing him.

How can we explain away cases such as these? And what are the odds of the following extraordinary set of coincidental facts?

The *Titan* was a totally fictional vessel which novelist Morgan Robertson used as the centrepiece of his book *Futility* in 1898. The *Titan* was the biggest passenger ship ever built, was 'unsinkable', was full of wealthy passengers, was on her maiden voyage, struck an iceberg, had her hull torn open, and sank with unnecessarily high loss of life because there were insufficient lifeboats. Fourteen years later the *Titanic* sank in identical circumstances.

That is a true story of an incredible coincidence. But was it pure chance that linked the fictional *Titan* and the *Titanic* or something less explicable? Many people believe that there is not such thing as coincidence; they call it synchronicity and claim that coincidence is actually contrived by our own consciousness.

The psychoanalyst C J Jung was the man who coined the word in an attempt to explain coincidences by an 'acausal principle'. He said that synchronicity – or meaningful coincidence – should not surprise us. Jung presented the analogy of a fly sitting on the minute hand of a clock. Every time the hand points upwards a bell sounds – which the fly wrongly takes to be an amazing coincidence!

Author and philosopher Arthur Koestler wrote about the subject of coincidence and received the following letter from Anthony S. Clancy of Dublin:
'I was born on the 7th day of the week
7th month of the year
7th year of the century
7th child of a 7th child, and I have
7 brothers; that makes
7 sevens.

Anthony Clancy's coincidences still left him without a winner!

'On my 27th birthday, at a race meeting, when I looked at the card to pick a winner in the

7th race, the horse numbered

7 was called

7th heaven, with a handicap of

7 stone. The odds were

7 to one. I put

7 shillings on the horse. It finished

7th.

Koestler was also contacted by Dr Thomas Leonard, a professor of statistics at the University of Warwick, who told him the following story. A new professor was analysing the laws of probability to his students. He knew that the odds against a coin landing on its edge were in the region of 1,000 million to one. He took a coin out of his pocket, tossed it in the air and when it fell on the perfectly smooth floor it landed vertically on its edge.

Another experiment in 'acausal meaningful coincidence' was set up by psychic and author Alan Vaughan and a physicist who, through previous laboratory tests, had been shown to have high psychic abilities. The physicist threw a coin against a wall so that it bounced several times before landing. The scientist predicted which way up the coin would face. He made 33 predictions and was correct every time. The odds against that are 8.6 billion to one.

One amazing story is that of Jason Pegler from

Essex, who was walking down the street when he heard a pay-phone ringing. Normally Jason would have just ignored it. But on this day, something made him pick the phone up. Incredibly the call was for him.

Even stranger was the fact that the number had been dialled by mistake. His work colleagues had been trying to contact Jason at home but had accidently dialled his pay-roll number by mistake. It just happened to be the number of the pay-phone Jason was passing right at that moment.

Jason Pegler's story was told on a 1996 television documentary which studied the phenomenon of coincidence. The programme's director, Jeremy Phillips, said: 'The number dialled had seven digits and there are 999,999 other numbers that could have been dialled. But there's no way of working out the odds of Jason walking past a phone box right at that moment.'

It's all down to what experts call large number theory - that someone is bound to have something strange happening to them somewhere in the world at any one time.

As author J B Priestley wrote: 'The future can be seen, and because it can be seen it can be changed.' If that is true, then coincidence might be the clue to a revolutionary new understanding of our destinies.

THE *MARY CELESTE*

She emerged as no more than a speck on the horizon. The crew of the *Dei Gratia* looked out to sea from time to time as she grew closer and her shape clearer. She was a two-masted, square-rigged brigantine, just like the *Dei Gratia* – but something was wrong about her.

The *Dei Gratia* gained steadily on the strange ship throughout a long, hot day until the two vessels were parallel.

By afternoon, the fascinated crew of the *Dei Gratia* took turns to examine the mysterious vessel as she wove her way erratically through the swell of the Atlantic. The deck of the *Dei Gratia* was by now crowded. The deck of the other vessel was entirely deserted.

Through his spyglass, Captain David Morehouse examined the brigantine from bow to stern. The ship was lurching through the water in an ungainly fashion and Morehouse found it difficult to keep his eye focused on the strange scene. He saw that she had only two of her sails set, the others being still furled or ripped to tatters. There was not a soul in sight. No one was at the wheel. There was no sign of life whatsoever.

Morehouse aimed his eyeglass at the bow and

One of the great unsolved mysteries of all time - the
Mary Celeste.

focussed on the ship's nameplate. It read: *Mary Celeste*.

The *Mary Celeste*, built at Spencer Island, Nova Scotia, was launched in 1861 as the *Amazon* and immediately hit a series of mishaps. Her first skipper fell ill and died on the eve of her maiden voyage. His replacement ran her into a fishing boat on her maiden voyage and the brig had to return to port for repairs. In dock, a fire broke out.

On her first Atlantic crossing, the jinx seemed to have been lifted. But as the *Amazon* entered the Straits of Dover, she collided with another brig, which sank. Again patched up, the *Amazon* returned to Nova Scotia where she promptly ran aground on a sandbank.

This time the owners had run out of patience. The ship was sold several times and ended up with a New York consortium who renamed her the *Mary Celeste*. The name itself was reputedly a mistake. The signwriter was supposed to have painted the word 'Marie' to match the spelling with the French 'Celeste'! (Ironically, 'Marie' is the name by which most people today incorrectly refer to her.)

And so it came to be that the *Mary Celeste* set sail from New York's Staten Island on 7 November 1872 under the captaincy of Benjamin Spooner Briggs. This proud, puritanic, teetotal, Massachusetts mariner had hired an experienced crew of mate, second mate, cook and four seamen.

Captain Benjamin Spooner Briggs.

Also aboard were Captain Briggs's wife Sarah and one of their children, two-year-old Sophia, leaving an elder son at home. The cargo was 1,700 barrels of denatured alcohol bound for Genoa, Italy.

Eight days later, on 15 November, the *Dei Gratia* also left New York, bound for Gibraltar with a cargo of petroleum. At 3pm on 5 December the two ships met at 38° 20' north latitude, 17° 50' west longitude, about 645km (400 miles) west of Lisbon.

Having hailed the *Mary Celeste* without result, Captain Morehouse ordered the ship's boat launched, and first mate Oliver Deveau, second mate John Wright and crewman John Johnson rowed across to the mystery brig.

While Johnson remained in the boat, the other two men hauled themselves over the rails and for an hour searched the boat for any sign of life. There was none.

The rigging, seemingly battered by a storm, flapped in the wind. The jib, fore-topmast staysail and fore-lower topsail were all set; but the foresail and the upper foresail had been blown away and other sails were either still furled or in shreds. The binnacle had been knocked over, the compass lying smashed on the deck. The wheel spun freely. The cargo hatches were still securely battened, although water slopped in and out of an open galley door.

Below decks, the scene was even more eerie. In

Sarah Briggs.

the galley, preparations seemed to have been made for a meal, although nothing had been served. (Later stories that a meal had been set and the plates were still warm are fiction.) In the crew's quarters, clothes lay on bunks and washing hung from lines. In the mate's cabin was a chart showing the position of the *Mary Celeste* up to 24 November.

In the captain's cabin, a melodeon belonging to Mrs Briggs still had a sheet of music in it. A sewing machine lay on a table. Daughter Sophie's toys were undisturbed. On another table lay the log of Captain Benjamin Spooner Briggs. It read:

'Monday, 25th. At five o'clock made island of St Mary's bearing E-SE. At eight o'clock, Eastern Point bore S-SW six miles distant.'

As fascinating as these discoveries were, more telling were the items that were missing from the ship: the sextant, chronometer, navigation book, bill of lading – and the ship's small boat. A length of railing had been broken off where the boat had been lowered over the side.

When the crewmen of the *Dei Gratia* returned from their inspection, they and Captain Morehouse debated what could have caused the abandonment of the brigantine. The crew had launched the small yawl and fled the safety of their ship. But why?

• Had the *Mary Celeste* been abandoned in a storm? If so, why was there so little storm damage aboard? Crew crockery and the captain's fine bone china was unbroken. A bottle of cough medicine stood uncorked and unspilled on a table.

• Had there been a mutiny? Why then would the mutineers abandon ship along with the captain? In any case, there had been no sign of a struggle.

• Had the crew gone on a drunken rampage? True, as it was discovered later, nine of the alcohol casks in the hold were empty. But, as Deveau affirmed, the cargo hatches were perfectly battened down. And Captain Briggs was a strictly teetotal puritan who would not have countenanced drink being consumed on his ship. In any case, the cargo was denatured alcohol, which would have given the crew acute pains before they could have drunk enough to become intoxicated.

• Had the ship been taking in water? A sounding rod was found on deck and there was three feet of water in the hold. But that was no more than any old wooden brig would have taken in over such a voyage and could easily have been pumped out.

All these speculations were to remain unanswered. An even greater mystery, however, was how the ship had managed to keep on course without a crew for 10 days and 800km (500 miles). When the *Dei Gratia* had come alongside the *Mary Celeste*, the former had her sails set on a port tack while the latter was on a starboard tack. There was no way that the *Mary Celeste* could have travelled the entire course she had with her sails set that way. Someone had been on board after the last log entry of 25 November.

With these questions unanswered, Captain Morehouse put three of his men aboard the *Mary Celeste* and sailed with her to Gibraltar, where he claimed her as salvage reward. There he had to argue with the colony's bumbling Attorney General, Frederick Solly Flood, who at first accused the captain of being a conspirator with the missing Briggs in a plot to abandon the *Mary Celeste* in order to extort salvage money from her owners. His next ludicrous suggestion was that Morehouse himself had slaughtered the crew.

Eventually Captain Morehouse and his men were granted the inadequate sum of £1,700 – a fraction of the ship's worth – and the *Mary Celeste*, under a new crew, was allowed to continue her voyage to Genoa to offload her cargo before returning to the United States.

Over the next 11 years, the *Mary Celeste* changed hands no fewer than 17 times. She was considered a jinxed ship, and none of her new owners would keep her for long. She sailed up and down America's eastern seaboard, losing crew and cargo alike, and suffering mishaps from collisions to shipboard fires.

In 1884 her final owners overinsured her and sent her to Haiti where, in the calmest of seas and with the clearest visibility, she ran aground! The conspirators were brought to court but the poor *Mary Celeste* rotted away forgotten on a coral reef.

JINXES

Can objects become jinxed by a force from beyond the grave – so that the people who come into contact with them suffer misfortune and death? What causes a ship or a motorcar, manufactured in the same way as numerous others, to become eternally damned to back luck, and sometimes worse?

Are the tales of jinxes handed down through the years the result of overactive imaginations?

Or can the unfortunate dead still exert a mysterious force on the living?

Of all jinxed objects, few can have bestowed more misery than a motorcar owned by the Hapsburg dynasty of imperial Austria.

The open-topped limousine was given to the Archduke Franz Ferdinand, heir to the troubled throne. He rode it in July 1914 on a state visit to Sarajevo, in Bosnia-Herzegovina, at that time a part of the Austro-Hungarian empire. In the car with the archduke on this ill-fated day were his wife, General Potiorek of the Austrian army, three other dignitaries and a driver.

A fervent young nationalist called Gavrilo Princip stepped in front of the vehicle on its official tour of the city and shot the archduke and his wife,

Archduchess Sophie. The event was to trigger the First World War.

General Potiorek became the car's next owner. Several weeks into the war, his armies suffered a rout at the hands of the ill-organised soldiers of Serbia, and the general was summoned back to Vienna by the Emperor Franz Joseph I. There in the capital, his reputation ruined, his sanity destroyed, he died.

A captain on Potiorek's staff took charge of the jinxed vehicle. Nine days later, in a terrible accident, he killed two peasants on the road before swerving into a tree and killing himself.

After the war, the governor of the newly independent Yugoslavia took charge of the car and endured a succession of terrible accidents, one of which cost him his left arm. The car was then sold to a doctor, who was crushed to death when he overturned it into a ditch. The next owner was Simon Manthrides, a diamond dealer. He fell to his death from a precipice.

The car passed into the hands of a Swiss racing driver who killed himself in an accident while driving it. The next owner – and victim – was a rich Serbian farmer.

He paid an unknown but reputedly fabulous sum for the vehicle, which had by now acquired great historical value. One morning, the engine would not turn over, so he ordered one his farm hands to tow him with a horse and cart. Unfortunately, the owner forgot to turn off the ignition and the engine started suddenly. The car lurched forward into the cart, overturning it and killing the farmer.

Finally, a garage owner lost his life in the car while returning from a wedding. He had tried to overtake a long line of vehicles but was killed as the car spun out of control.

The car now rests harmlessly in a Viennese museum. It is never taken out on the road.

Was it a jinx that made one woman suffer three of the worst shipwrecks of the 20th century? Or was it luck – plain good luck that she survived all three Atlantic disasters?

In 1915 Mrs Joan Murray was aboard the *Lusitania*, a ship torpedoed by the Germans off the Irish coast, with great loss of life. She survived that horror, counting herself lucky, as she had already been one of the survivors of history's greatest shipwreck three years earlier, when the *Titanic* hit an iceberg. In 1927 she escaped with her life once more when she survived a collision in the Atlantic between the *Celtic* and the *Anaconda*.

One man jinxed – or blessed, depending on one's point of view – must certainly be Wesley MacIntyre, who was plunged into a string deadly situations, only to emerge miraculously with his life every time.

During the Second World War he dived off his US warship just before it was bombed and many of his crewmates were killed. In 1950 he managed to steer his runaway truck without brakes for almost three kilometres down a mountain road, finally bringing it to a stop in a parking area by spinning it round and round.

In 1959 he had an accident in a lorry loaded with explosive gas but it failed to ignite. In another accident he was saved by a mattress which took the full impact of a blast when the air tanks for his truck's braking system exploded.

Finally MacIntyre was the sole survivor of a catastrophe which killed 35 people. He was thrown into the water when a ship accidentally rammed the Sunshine Skyway Bridge across the mouth of Tampa Bay, Florida. 'The Good Lord must certainly be saving something up for me,' he quipped as he was taken away on a stretcher.

It is not only large objects that can bring a jinx upon those connected with them. Take the case of the small 'good luck' charm purchased by a middle-aged English couple in 1928...

Charles and Mary Lambert spotted a small figurine of an Oriental monk in a shop window in Kobe, Japan, and went in to inquire its price. They examined the figure in detail and found it to be made of flawless ivory. When told the cost, it seemed too low to be true, so they paid for it and departed swiftly, unable to believe their luck.

The figure was of Ho-tei, a 6th Buddhist monk whose life was devoted to helping others, particularly unfortunate children. He was later promoted to the status of a god, and smiling figures of the monk can still be bought in the Far East as tokens of good luck.

This was to be no good luck charm for Mr and Mrs Lambert, however. It was jinxed to bring them bad luck. And their catalogue of woe began almost as soon as they had boarded their ship for the voyage home to England.

On the second day out, as the ship was heading for its next port of call, Manila in the Philippines, Mrs Lambert contracted a violent toothache. Medicine prescribed by the ship's doctor did little to ease it.

Once in Manila, the pair of them were brought down with a fever which caused them pain in every joint. Mrs Lambert visited a dentist in the city who mistakenly cut through a tooth nerve, causing her even more intense pain.

Mr Lambert did not notice that his wife had swapped the figurine from her suitcase to his for the next leg of the journey, to Australia. And this time it was Mr Lambert who came down with raging toothache. When he went to a dentist in Sydney, he instructed him to 'pull and keep pulling' all his teeth until the pain went away.

Their next stop was Auckland, New Zealand, where their luggage was parted from them and their tooth pains subsided. When their cases were returned to their new cabin, however, new and agonising pangs of toothache began all over again.

Setting sail across the Pacific, the Lamberts loaned the ivory statuette to another woman passenger who had expressed a particular interest in figurines. She kept it for the night and handed it back to the Lamberts the next morning – saying that she and her husband had both spent a restless night with toothache.

In the United States, the English couple wanted to make a gift of the Ho-tei to Charles Lambert's mother, who expressed herself 'utterly enchanted' with the little smiling Buddha. As she examined it, however, she noticed in the base of the figure a small hole which had been neatly plugged with a tiny ivory stopper. Sensing that it contained 'bad medicine', she declined the gift.

The Lamberts were not at all superstitious. Yet they now realised that, although they were in possession of something that was supposed to bring good luck, for some reason it was bringing pain and discomfort. In trepidation of worse things to come, the Lamberts sold the Ho-tei to a London antique dealer – whose verdict was that it had been plundered from a temple.

Perhaps the robbers had unleashed a vengeful

curse when they removed the Buddha from the sanctity of its proper resting place.

GLORIA RAMIREZ

It was a busy Saturday evening at the Riverside General Hospital when a 31-year-old woman was brought to the casualty department suffering from chest pains. Shortly after her arrival, she began gasping for air. Her severe breathing problems worsened and she was admitted to the hospital for treatment.

As nursing staff prepared her for a series of tests, the woman collapsed from an acute cardiac arrest. Exactly 36 minutes after being admitted she was now the subject of a full-blown emergency. Death would follow within the hour.

This was how the life-or-death drama of Gloria Ramirez had begun. By the time it ended shortly afterwards, the woman would be the subject of one of the weirdest medical mysteries of all time. For never before in the annals of medical history have doctors been knocked unconscious themselves – by fumes seeping from a dying patient.

Exactly how 31-year-old Gloria Ramirez, of Riverside, Los Angeles, became a human gas chamber is likely to remain an enigma. So is the fact that while some nurses attending to her passed out, others carried on with their work unaffected. The case adds up to an account stranger than the weirdest plot of any sci-fi B-movie of the 1950s.

When Ramirez arrived at the Riverside General Hospital on 19 February 1994, she was not only complaining of chest pains and breathing problems, she also confirmed to nurses that she was suffering from cervical cancer. As a consequence of this, she was taking pain killers and the anti-nausea drug Compazine.

Nurse Susan Kane was one of the first of the medical staff to attend to Ramirez – and one of the first to succumb. She had been taking a blood sample when she noticed a smell like ammonia coming from the patient. The blood in her syringe also seemed to have been contaminated with tiny yellow or white-coloured flecks.

Overcome by the gas, Nurse Kane collapsed. Dr Julie Gorchynski immediately took her place but then passed out as well. Seconds later the respiratory therapist, Maureen Welsh, keeled over, followed by nurse Sally Balderas and another of her colleagues.

The emergency room was by now beginning to look as though a bomb had hit it. Yet, curiously, not every member of the medical staff was affected. Dr Humberto Ochoa didn't even notice the fumes as he worked on frantically to save not only his patient but his own colleagues.

Worst affected was his fellow doctor, Julie Gorchynski. She was rushed to Loma Linda

University Medical Center, Los Angeles, where for a week she remained in intensive care at as scientists tried to understand what had happened to her body. Dr Gorchynski was suffering breathing problems and muscle spasms, conditions which lingered for months afterwards. In April she had to undergo major surgery to save her knees. The bones were somehow being starved of oxygen.

The other medic badly affected, Nurse Balderas, suffered intense headaches, sleep deprivation, stomachache and vomiting. Both she and Dr Gorchynski were diagnosed 'sleep apnea' victims, a condition in which breathing stops temporarily.

Senior doctors and poisons experts had to wait until Balderas and her friends had sufficiently recovered before they could interrogate them about what had occurred in the emergency room. Balderas told the baffled researchers: 'The woman had this film on her body, like you see on the ground at a gas station.'

Tests indicated that the victims had suffered organophosphate poisoning. There were the same white and yellow crystals present in their bodies as had been reported in Ramirez's blood sample. But this conclusion produced more questions than it solved.

For a start, Ramirez had not taken organophosphates as far as anyone could tell. Her family emphasised that whatever pain she had been in from cancer, she would never have taken poison. She would never have committed suicide. She would never have abandoned her two children.

The senior medical coordinator for California's Department of Food and Agriculture, Peter H. Kurtz, said: 'I know of no organophosphate in use today that would cause the kinds of things reported in that hospital.'

The postmortem examination on Gloria Ramirez took place on 24 February under the most extraordinary conditions. Pathologists treated the body of the unfortunate Gloria almost as though they were dealing with an alien from outer space.

The pathology team wore anti-chemical warfare suits and gas masks, breathing apparatus and two-way radios. A mini television camera, air samplers and sensors were poked into the body bag before it was lifted out of its air-tight aluminium coffin. All medical staff were prohibited from working longer than a 30-minute shift inside the morgue.

The stated, medical cause of death – cardiac arrest caused by kidney failure, in turn caused by cancer – shed little light on the mystery. Unable to explain the bizarre events, the local coroner's office resorted to the hopelessly unscientific and inadequate explanation that fumes emanating from Ramirez's body were nothing more than the 'smell of death'.

Just about the only believable theory submitted came from Los Angeles Police Department sources. They allege that Ramirez was a some-time drug user who got her kicks from phencyclidine (PCP), also known as 'angel dust'. This anaesthetic compound is manufactured in illegal laboratories across the California. Ramirez was known to frequent one of them.

Had she experimented by rubbing one of the chemicals used in PCP manufacture on her body, perhaps by first dissolving it in dimethyl sulfoxide (DMSO)? This liquid used as a solvent has the characteristic of smelling differently depending on the body tissue of the user. It is used principally to draw substances into the bloodstream through the skin.

The use of DMSO might just explain the film on Gloria Ramirez's skin and the strong smell of ammonia. But it is a theory supported by few hard facts, and the mystery of the 'human gas chamber' looks likely to last many years yet.

TELEPORTATION AND VANISHMENTS

Peter Stuart Ney was a French teacher in the town of Florence, South Carolina. A quiet but popular member of the community, he gained notoriety only on his deathbed in 1846 when he announced weakly: 'I am France's Marshal Ney.'

The puzzle was that Marshal Michel Ney, who had been one of Napoleon Bonaparte's most able generals, had been executed 31 years earlier. He had faced a firing squad in Paris in 1815 following Napoleon's defeat at Waterloo.

No one believed the teacher's story until a doctor examined scars on his body and checked them against records of Marshal Ney's war wounds. Later a leading handwriting expert of the day, David Carvalho, of New York, compared documents written by the general and the teacher – and pronounced the authors to be one and the same.

Peter Stuart Ney was a victim – or perhaps a happy beneficiary – of what is known by psychic researchers as the twin phenomena of 'teleportation' and 'vanishment'.

'Vanishment' is the label given to cases of people who quite simply vanish altogether! And the only explanation ever put forward is that they are the victims of some time-slip or warp which literally whisks their earthly bodies away into the ether forever, never to be seen again.

One of the strangest of such cases was that of an old cripple named Owen Parfitt, who vanished from outside his home in 1769. He was sitting at the door of his home in Somerset, unable to move because he had been paralysed by a stroke. His cousin went into the house for one minute, reemerging to find Parfitt's rug on the chair, but Parfitt himself gone. There had been no one near the isolated country house. He had vanished into thin air.

The most famous 'vanishment' of all time was that of British diplomat Benjamin Bathurst in 1809. On his return journey to Hamburg following a mission to the Austrian court, Bathurst stopped for dinner at an inn at the town of Perleberg. After the meal, he and his companion returned to their waiting coach. The friend watched as Bathurst walked towards the front of the coach to examine the horses – and disappear never to be seen again.

Vanishing tricks do not require the atmosphere of old coaches and murky country nights. In 1975 Jackson Wright was driving his wife Martha from New Jersey to New York City. Once through the Lincoln Tunnel, Jackson drew up to wipe the windshield while Martha cleared the back window. When he looked round, she had disappeared.

The most dramatic disappearance of all, however, was reported by three old soldiers who came forward 50 years after the fateful Gallipoli campaign of the First World War. The three, members of a New Zealand field company, said that, from a clear vantage point, they had observed a battalion of the Royal Norfolk Regiment marching up a hillside in Suvla Bay, Turkey, on 21 August 1915 (some accounts have it as 12 August). According to the New Zealanders' account, the column of English soldiers approached a strange, small, low-lying cloud...

'When they arrived at this cloud, they marched straight into it with no hesitation, but no one ever came out. About an hour later, after the last of the file had disappeared into it, this cloud very unobtrusively lifted off the ground and rose slowly to join other clouds... On Turkey surrendering in 1918, Britain demanded the return of this regiment. Turkey replied that she had neither captured it nor made contact with it, and did not know it existed.'

Although the memories of the old soldiers who recounted this story may have faded, it has been established that most of the 1st/5th Royal Norfolks disappeared on 12 August 1915. Only some of their bodies were ever found.

Some believers in the strange phenomena of 'vanishment' and 'teleportation' theorise that time may 'slip', enabling events and distance to be telescoped together. Others believe that the universe may contain strange cosmic whirlpools which draw people irresistibly into them and move them at will to anywhere on the planet. Or possibly whisk them away into another dimension altogether...

Cases of 'teleportation' are only slightly less frightening than 'vanishment'. In the language of the psychic researchers, 'teleportation' is the name given to the mysterious phenomenon of people who move through time and space.

In 1593 one of the earliest recorded instances of this extraordinary feat occurred. A troop of soldiers assembled in the plaza in front of the Grand Palace in Mexico City were suddenly joined by one further soldier, dressed in the strangest of uniforms. Asked where he was from, he said that he had been ordered to guard the governor's palace in Manila - half way round the world in the Philippines.

Asked why, the man answered that the governor had been murdered the night before and the city was in unrest. As puzzled as his interrogators, the stranger said in Spanish: 'I now see this is not the governor's palace, so evidently I am not in Manila. But here I am and this is a palace and so I am doing my duty as nearly as is possible.'

The stranger was thrown into jail. He was swiftly released two months later, however, when a ship arrived in Mexico from the Philippines with the news that the governor there had been killed on the very night the soldier had said. The mystery man took ship back to the Philippines and was never heard of again.

In 1655 a man was at his work in Goa, India, when he was swept into the air to find himself in Portugal, the native land he had left more than 20 years before. Unfortunately for him, the all-powerful servants of the Inquisition rewarded his unwanted and unimaginable trip with death, by burning him at the stake because he was guilty of a crime 'against the godly order of things.'

Another case of which the church took a dim view was that of Sister Mary, of Agreda in Spain, who outraged clerics of the time with her tales of flights between Europe and the Americas, where she claimed to be spreading Christianity to the heathen natives. This was said to have occurred between the years 1620 and 1631, but all she received for her revelations was scorn.

Credence was only given to the story when a priest who was officially charged with converting the natives to Christianity reported back to Spain. Father Alonzo de Benavides wrote to both the Pope and King Philip IV of Spain complaining that his missionary work there was pointless; someone had beaten him to it.

He said: 'A mysterious nun, dressed in blue, has been here. She distributes rosaries and crosses and bears a chalice to celebrate the holy mass.'

Upon his return to Spain, Father Benavides interviewed Sister Mary at length and fully supported her claim that she took these mysterious flights to Central America. She was able to supply astonishing details of people and and places, although her superiors testified that she had never left their convent. A later biographer wrote:

'That Mary really visited America is attested to by the logs of the Spanish conquistadors, the French explorers, the identical accounts by different tribes of Indians a thousand miles apart. Every authentic history of the southwest of the United States records this mystic phenomenon unparalleled in the entire history of the world.'

A more recent – and well documented case – of 'teleportation' occurred in Providence, Rhode Island, on 17 January 1887. That was the day when Ansel Bourne walked from his home to a nearby bank, drew out $551 and set out to visit a nephew who lived nearby and with whom he was planning to buy some farmland. Fifty-six days later – on 14 March – he woke up in bed in a room above a general store in Norriston, Pennsylvania.

Bourne, who was a carpenter and preacher, could recall leaving his nephew's home but had no idea what he was doing 370km (230 miles) away in Pennsylvania. The first person he could find, his landlord, explained to him that he was now Mr A J Brown. In that character, he had rented the business in early February and had run the store successfully ever since. He was a pillar of the community and attended the local Methodist church.

Puzzled as to why he should take the trouble of setting up a business in which he had neither experience nor even any interest, Bourne allowed himself to be hypnotised by a Harvard professor, William James. Under hypnosis, he said he was Albert John Brown and described running the Pennsylvania store – but could recall nothing whatsoever of his 'real' life as Ansel Bourne. Professor James's findings were that Bourne and Brown were two distinctly different people, each having his own mannerisms – and even his own, individual handwriting!

HEAVEN

Throughout this book, we have looked at examples of life beyond the grave that are sometimes weird and wonderful, sometimes frightening or plain evil. If these stories are evidence of after-death existence, then the ultimate mystery must be examined: is there a Heaven – and perhaps even a Hell?

Heaven is an idea that has intrigued man since he first walked the Earth. It is such an attractive prospect, living forever in a perfect paradise, that many dismiss it as wishful thinking. But today modern medical techniques mean more and more people are being revived after having taken a look behind death's door. Many of them believe they have been to Heaven – and they paint a remarkable picture of what they have seen.

Doctor Tom Smith, medical adviser to the British medical journal *Pulse*, made a study of patients' reports of the hereafter. In it he said: 'Their accounts have remarkable similarities. They begin by floating above their bodies, watching what is going on below. Then they talk of travelling down some sort of tunnel with a light at the end. They all speak of a bright light, of great joy, of someone they know coming to meet them.'

Since, by the nature of their experiences, there can never be tangible proof of the existence of a heavenly afterlife, the only evidence must be in the words of those who believe they have been there.

• Leonard Bruce was 24 when he was taken into hospital in Louisville, Kentucky, for his seventh cancer operation. He believed it would be his last – and, after eight years of painful surgery on his throat, he was not unhappy about the prospect of death. He says:

'I wanted to die. I felt relief that this was going to be my last operation. After eight hours, the anaesthetic was wearing off and the nurses were waiting for me to come round. But I didn't want to.

'I closed my eyes and waited for death. Suddenly I was floating in mid air, looking down at my body lying on the wheeled hospital cart. All around me doctors and nurses were working frantically. I actually said goodbye to my body as I turned away towards a bright light. I felt relaxed, out of pain and really happy for the first time in years.

'I felt, rather than saw, people around me. Somehow I knew they were my friends. They seemed to be drawing me along with them into the clouds. Then I felt something stop me dead in my tracks. A male voice, authoritative but mellow, commanded, "Do not go further, my son – I have things for your to do".

'I opened my eyes and the first thing I saw was

a nurse, her hand to her mouth in amazement, saying, "He's back! He's awake!".'

Leonard adds: 'My friends nowadays ask me why I am so calm and why I don't worry. I tell them with a smile that it is because I do not fear death. I have been to Heaven once; and it's a wonderful place.'

• Housewife Betty Maltz died for 28 minutes from peritonitis after an operation. She says: 'I clearly heard one of the doctors say, "She's dead." The next instant I was on a roller-coaster, soaring up to a very high point. In hospital I had been in a lot of pain but now it had gone.

'I found myself walking up a steep hill and through a meadow of beautiful flowers. It was like a lovely spring day. I was walking towards a brilliant yellow light. Then I heard my father saying, "Oh Jesus." I could see him and my mother beside my hospital bed. I turned away from the light and walked across the meadow, back to my body.'

Betty, of South Dakota, remembers sitting up in her hospital bed and pulling the sheet off her face. She says: 'A nursing assistant took one look and ran out shouting "It's a ghost!".'

• Owen Thomas was 20 years of age when he was stabbed through the heart while trying to help a friend being attacked in New York in 1981. When he was brought in to Beekman Downtown Hospital's emergency room he had no blood pressure, no pulse, no heartbeat. He was clinically dead for five minutes as surgeons began trying to stitch up his wounds. He says: 'I knew I was dead. But I was approached, as if in a dream, by my brother Christopher who had died 20 years earlier. He put his hands on me, pushed me away and said, "We don't want you." Then I returned.'

• In England, Edmund Wilbourne died for 30 minutes from pneumonia and pleurisy when he was a young man in the 1950s. Wilbourne, an officer in the Church Army, recalls his brief time in Heaven thus:

'I seemed to be whirled round and round and when I stopped I was in a place of beauty and light. I met my mother, who had died when I was four, and I recognised several other people. A man who had once been my Sunday school teacher came to meet me and said he would show me round. I even met Jesus, and I remember I made a joke about the nail prints in his hands and feet being the only man-made things in Heaven. He smiled. Then an old woman's voice said, "Please don't let him go yet." Jesus seemed to give me a push, and I woke up on a mortuary slab in my nightshirt. I later found out that the old woman I had heard had in fact been my landlady in Manchester, who had prayed for me.'

Mr Wilbourne is absolutely certain that he went to Heaven. 'It was definitely not a dream or hallucination,' he says firmly. 'The people I saw were as real as the people I see in the street. Although I was physically dead, I felt full of life.'

• Barney Hayden, a Bristol publican, was revived with electric shocks after dying from a heart attack. He says: 'I seemed to be floating in the air, looking down at the doctors trying to save my life. Then I found myself in a beautiful garden full of trees and flowers. My father, who had died 15 years earlier, was there. He was standing in front of a door in the garden wall which seemed to lead into a long corridor. He said, "Don't come in yet, It's too soon." Next thing I knew I was opening my eyes in hospital.'

• Being met by close relatives 'on the other side' is a common theme in such cases. In New York, a victim of a knife attack claims he went to Heaven, where he also met his mother. Lawrie McPherson was stabbed through the heart by a mugger in 1980 and was clinically dead when he arrived at hospital. Doctors managed to revive him, however. McPherson says: 'There were all these lights and it was so hot. I got to heaven and my mother, who died when I was 10, was standing there. She told me to go back.'

• Martin Ford, the tough, no-nonsense foreman of a California timber factory, was dead for 30 minutes after a heart attack in 1971. He felt elated as his spirit left his body at the start of his deadly experience. He says:

'I felt weightless. Faster and faster I travelled until ahead of me I began to see iridescent lights beckoning me. I was looking down on a beautiful city on a hill from a great height. It was the most beautiful place I had ever seen. As I came closer I saw millions of shimmering lights, and one central, powerful light that was the source of all the others. I had a conversation with this light, which I am certain was the Lord. We didn't use words. It was more of a feeling. Then I felt something tugging me and I was back in my body.'

• Helen Nelson died for three minutes in hospital after suffering a heart attack at her home in Connecticut. She says: 'I heard a doctor shout, "We're going to lose her." Then I was moving very fast through a dark, cylindrical void. Far, far away I could see a light. When I reached it there were pillars and stairs made of marble. My parents suddenly appeared, and they looked just as they did before they died years ago. They held up their hands to me and I felt full of joy and peace. Then my father said, "Helen you must go back. It is not time." Suddenly I felt a painful tug and saw brilliant flashes of light. Then I saw the doctors around me.'

• Marti Hampton died in a Dallas hospital while giving birth to her second child. 'I left my body,' she says. 'I was a cloud over the operating table, but before I knew it I was in Heaven. Hands reached out to me and a voice said, "Come my child, your baby boy did not die. You are not bound for Hell." I loved Heaven but I saw hardships for my children if I did not go back. When I opened my eyes I was back in hospital.'

• New York executive John Migliaccio was revived by the kiss of life after drowning in a diving accident off the coast of New Jersey. He says: 'I had this feeling of exhaustion and my arms were like lead – when suddenly I felt light and free. I was like an eyeball in the sky looking down at my body in the water. I must have been very high because I could see up and down the coast for miles. I was flying around at will when suddenly I was hovering just above my body. Then I was lying on the beach gasping for breath.'

• Durdana Khan was only two in 1966 when she died for 20 minutes from a brain virus. But she has crystal clear recollections of the world beyond before being revived by her doctor father in Norwood, South London. She says:

'It was very bright and there were other people there. I met my grandfather and his mother and my grandmother. Both had died long before I was born, but I recognised them later from photographs. I remember hearing my father ask me to come back, and I told my grandfather that I wanted to. He said he would have to ask the Lord. He took my hand and we went to see Him. All I remember of God is a bright shining light. The next thing I knew I was on my father's bed. I am certainly not afraid of dying now that I know what it is like when you do.'

• Louise Walters, of North Carolina, died briefly after a serious operation. She says: 'I saw a vision of a bridge with sunlight pouring over it. On the other side was my father who had died long before. He gestured to me to come over the bridge and join him. He was smiling and very happy. I'm sure he was talking to me from the next world.'

• Mary Cilenti, of Long Island, died when her lung collapsed during minor surgery. 'I remember walking through a long, dark tunnel,' she says, 'when all of a sudden I saw a light on my left. As I walked towards it I could see my patron saint, Mother Frances Cabrini.'

Cilenti pleaded with Mother Cabrini to let her return to her body so that she could take care of her baby daughter. 'Mother Cabrini smiled at me and nodded. I understood what she meant – and that moment I became aware of doctors pounding my chest as they revived me.'

• Film star Donald Sutherland believes he has glimpsed life beyond the grave. It happened when he was critically ill with spinal meningitis while filming *Kelly's Heroes* in former Yugoslavia in the mid-1970s. He says:

'I was in a bad way. I was sinking fast with a raging fever, and the doctors seemed to have given up hope for me. Then the fever, the pain and the acute distress seemed to evaporate. I was floating above my body, surrounded by a soft, blue light. I began to glide down a long tunnel, slipping farther and farther away from the bed. Suddenly, I found myself back in my body, and from then on I recovered very quickly. Afterwards, the doctors told me that I had actually died for a short time.'

• Some victims suffer not only death but a battle for their souls once they cross into the life beyond. Harry Wood was attending a football game in Chattanooga, Tennessee, in 1981 when he keeled over with a heart attack. As he was rushed to hospital, he was swept into the limbo of the dead and into a terrifying struggle that was to change his life for ever. In the words of the 61-year-old retired maintenance engineer:

'I didn't know where I was but I knew where I was going. I was going to Hell! I was terrified. There were hundreds of spirits all around me and they were snarling and screaming in rage. I kept calling to them to help me but they were like wild animals, gnashing their teeth. They only had time for themselves.'

Harry says that he and the other spirits were not yet in Hell. They were deep in the earth – in a 'pit' that was veiled in mist. The ground was like volcanic ash and the trees were made of thorns.

'There was one spirit hovering beside me that stood out from the rest. It was evil and gave me a terrible feeling of being lost. I knew it was the Devil. There was another spirit near me. I didn't really see it; I was just aware of it. It was as if it was saying, "I'm here if you need me." I knew it would do nothing unless I asked for help.

'The other spirit, the Devil, was tugging at me, pulling me deeper and deeper. I knew it was pulling me into Hell. I was losing my soul to Satan.'

When Harry slipped into death, hospital officials summoned his wife Mary Sue to his bedside. 'As soon as I saw him I knew what was happening,' she says. 'He had no control over his eyes; they were fixed. I knew he was going into eternity. I whispered in his ear, "Harry, Jesus Christ is your only hope, honey – you have to call on Him".' Somehow her desperate appeal pierced the darkness that was engulfing Harry. He says:

'I screamed "Jesus help me" but I wasn't sincere. I still had my foolish pride. But I was getting weaker and weaker and I knew I was losing my fight with Satan. Finally I knew I was lost, and an icy terror washed over me. In desperation, I screamed again, "Jesus! Please help me!" This time I was truly sincere. Suddenly I was awake. Mary and my son Harry Jr were there. And I was alive.

'No one will ever know the terror I experienced. I don't know how long I was in that hellish place. But for me it was an eternity. It has changed my life completely.'

• Sixty-year-old Helen Womack, of Eugene, Oregon, was in hospital in 1974 for the fourth in a series of operations. This was how she described her experience: 'After the anaesthetic was administered, everything went blank for a while. Then there was a brilliant light and I was carried away.'

Helen found herself in a group of people and understood that it was her turn to give an account of her life. As I did, I became aware of the Devil standing on my left and Jesus standing on my right. I felt like a child between them.

'The Devil was beautiful. His garments were white and flowing. His face had a deep, mysterious, fascinating attraction. His hair was dark and flowing, his eyes dark and fathomless, and he had an air of controlled passion about him.

'I could hardly turn away from him but I finally turned my eyes to Jesus, and his eyes were filled with knowledge of all ages. Every virtue I have ever witnessed was there with him. Most of all I noticed a tender compassion and a twinkle of humour. My heart simply melted within me.'

The Devil told Helen that she had to choose and she cried out, '"Jesus, I love and trust you – we will all be with You." There was a loud blast, then I was standing with Jesus. I didn't want to come back to this world after seeing Him, but the Lord intended it. When I woke up in the recovery room I just cried and cried.'

Have all these people been to heaven – or even Hell? Medical men point out there could be another, much more down-to-earth explanation. As the brain loses oxygen, the outer parts die first. This could cause a tunnel effect and bright lights. The last part of the brain to die is the memory, which could carry on producing images of dead relatives.

But there is more evidence of a hereafter in the book *Life After Death*. Author Neville Randall reports the findings of mediums George Woods and Betty Greene, who believe they have taped conversations with dead people. Their work has been rigorously checked by independent experts to prove that the voices could not have been faked or the information fabricated.

The spirits talk of place with no conflicts and no worries, a place of flowers and peace. When someone dies, their spiritual self leaves the body and floats above it for a while, claims Randall. After a short period the dead person leaves the Earth and passes to the life beyond. But those who have been wicked on Earth have to work their way up through several levels before they reach Paradise itself, where they can no longer communicate with Earth. It is only those at the middle levels who can speak to those left on Earth. In Paradise everyone is in the prime of life. The old, the crippled and the ill are fit and young again. A 'newcomer' meets only the people he or she loved on Earth. Anyone who was unhappily married, for instance, does not meet his or her spouse – instead they might be reunited with a loved pet.

One psychic investigator, Sarah Estep, who holds a degree in education from the University of Virginia, says she has taped more than 15,000 messages from the dead since she began researching six years ago. From these she has built up a picture of what life after death is like.

'They say it's pretty and indicate that there are houses, but no food,' she says. 'They have said that you can be met by friends and loved ones who have also passed on if you want. Some voices have come through and said they are sick. Others have said they feel very good. They indicate there are doctors, nurses and healers over there'.

'It appears that when you die, you are met by spirit guides who are friends or loved ones. They have indicated that when they pass over to the other side, they sit with a guide and are gathered in a reception area. There are several different levels to which one might go, each better than the other.'

Heaven – a place of eternal happiness or the last hallucination of a dying brain? The mystery remains as deep as ever.